MW01174683

Assessment & Practice
Part 1 of 2

2.1

Contents

JUMP Math
250 The Esplanade, #408
Toronto, Ontario M5A 1J2
Canada
www.jumpmath.org

Writers: Dr. Francisco Kibedi, Dr. Anna Klebanov
Editors: Megan Burns, Natalie Francis, Lindsay Karpenko, Julie Takasaki, Liane Tsui,
         Susan Bindernagel, Jackie Dulson, Janice Dyer, Michelle MacAleese,
         Louise MacKenzie, Leanne Rancourt
Layout and Illustrations: Megan Blakes, Lorena González, Fely Guinasao-Fernandes, Linh Lam,
         Sawyer Paul, Nesba Yousef
Cover Design: Linh Lam, based on an original design by Blakeley Words+Pictures (2014)
Cover Photograph: © adriennexplores/Shutterstock

ISBN 978-1-77395-372-4

First printing June 2025

Printed and bound in Canada

To report an error or other issue in a JUMP Math resource, please visit our Corrections page at www.jumpmath.org.

Welcome to JUMP Math

Entering the world of JUMP Math means believing that every child has the capacity to be fully numerate and to love math. Founder and mathematician John Mighton has used this premise to develop his innovative teaching method. The resulting resources isolate and describe concepts so clearly and incrementally that everyone can understand them.

JUMP Math is comprised of Teacher Resources, Digital Lesson Slides, student Assessment & Practice Books, assessment tools, outreach programs, and professional development. All of this is presented on the JUMP Math website: **www.jumpmath.org**.

The Teacher Resource is available on the website for free use. Read the introduction to the Teacher Resource before you begin using these materials. This will ensure that you understand both the philosophy and the methodology of JUMP Math. The Assessment & Practice Books are designed for use by students, with adult guidance. Each student will have unique needs and it is important to provide the student with the appropriate support and encouragement as they work through the material.

Allow students to discover the concepts by themselves as much as possible. Mathematical discoveries can be made in small, incremental steps. The discovery of a new step is like untangling the parts of a puzzle. It is exciting and rewarding.

Students will need to answer the questions marked with a in a notebook. Grid paper notebooks should always be on hand for answering extra questions or when additional room for calculation is needed.

Contents

Unit 5: Geometry: 2-D Shapes

Unit 6: Probability and Data Management: Sorting and Graphing

Unit 7: Number Sense: Addition and Subtraction with Numbers to 100

Unit 8: Geometry: Symmetry

Unit 9: Number Sense: Equations and Word Problems

Unit 10: Number Sense: Using 10 to Add and Subtract

Unit 11: Measurement: More Length and Mass

PART 2
Unit 12: Number Sense: Skip Counting and Estimating

Unit 13: Number Sense: Addition Strategies

Unit 14: Number Sense: Subtraction Strategies

Unit 15: Patterns and Algebra: Growing and Shrinking Patterns

Unit 16: Geometry: 3-D Shapes

Unit 17: Number Sense: Money

Unit 18: Number Sense: Fractions, Multiplication, and Division

Unit 19: Measurement: Time

Unit 20: Probability and Data Management: Probability

Unit 21: Measurement: Area, Calendars, Temperature, and Capacity

Counting and Matching

 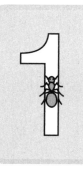   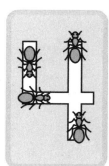 

☐ Colour.

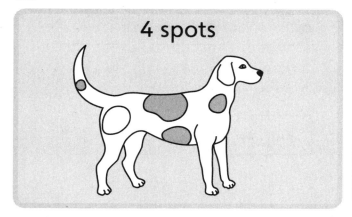

4 spots

1 spot

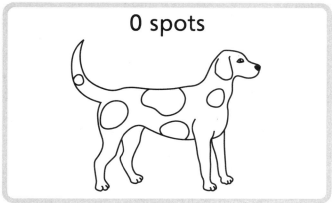

0 spots

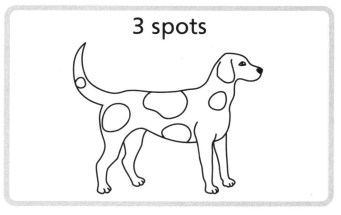

3 spots

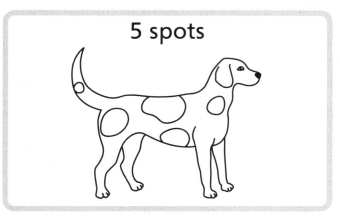

5 spots

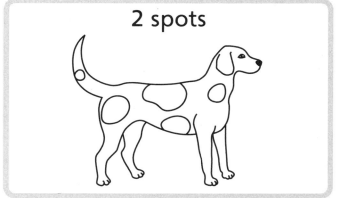

2 spots

◯ **Match by number.**

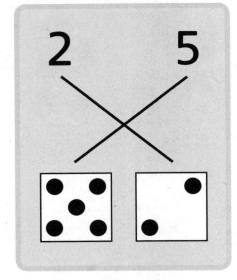

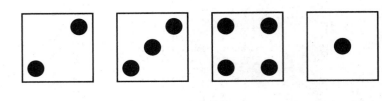

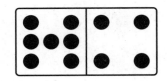 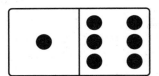 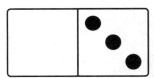 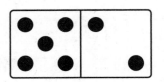

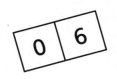 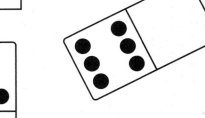 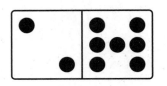 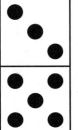 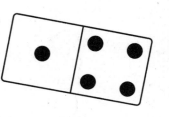

One-to-One Correspondence

☐ Circle the one that is **more**.

buttons   or   (holes)

people   or   chairs

people   or   chairs

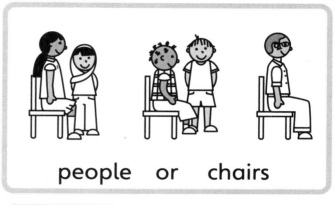

people   or   chairs

cups   or   straws

cups   or   straws

forks   or   plates

☐ Pair them up to find out which is **more**.

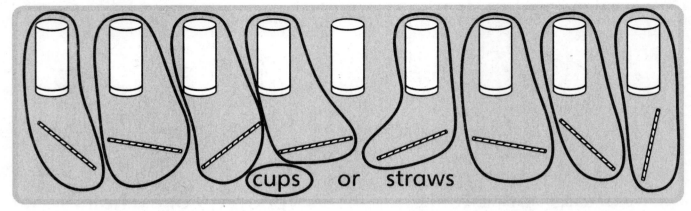

cups or straws

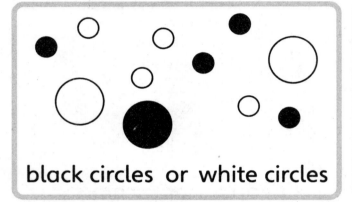

black circles or white circles

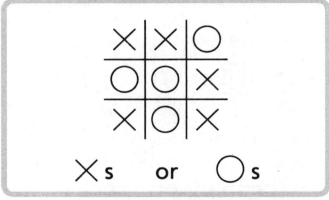

✕ s or ◯ s

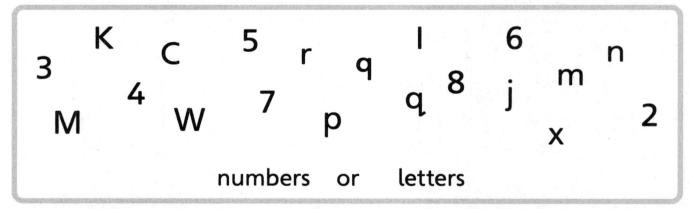

numbers or letters

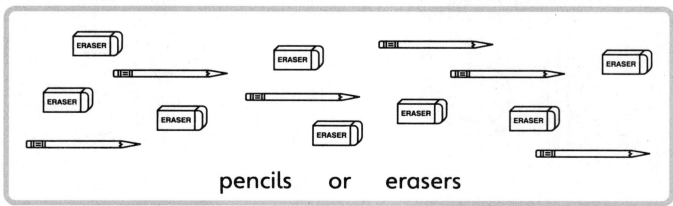

pencils or erasers

More, Fewer, and Less

How many ants?

1 2 3 4 5 6 7

There are __4__ ants.

1 2 3 4 5 6 7

There are _____ ants.

1 2 3 4 5 6 7

There are _____ ants.

1 2 3 4 5 6 7

There are _____ ants.

How many blocks?

| 1 | 2 | 3 | 4 | 5 | 6 | 7 | 8 | 9 | 10 |

There are _____ blocks.

| 1 | 2 | 3 | 4 | 5 | 6 | 7 | 8 | 9 | 10 |

There are _____ blocks.

| 1 | 2 | 3 | 4 | 5 | 6 | 7 | 8 | 9 | 10 |

There are _____ blocks.

☐ Trace the number of spiders.
☐ Trace the number of ants.
☐ Write **more**, **less**, or **fewer**.

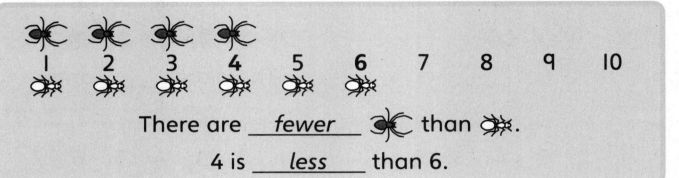

There are ___*fewer*___ 🕷 than 🐜.

4 is ___*less*___ than 6.

There are _____ 🕷 than 🐜.

7 is _____ than 5.

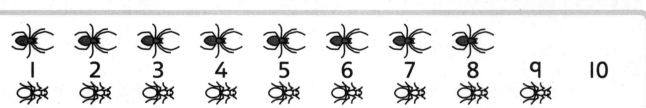

There are _____ 🕷 than 🐜.

8 is _____ than 9.

There are _____ 🕷 than 🐜.

10 is _____ than 7.

How Many More?

☐ Circle the **extras**.
☐ Write how many more.

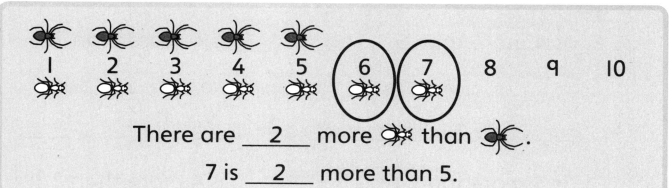

There are __2__ more 🐜 than 🕷.

7 is __2__ more than 5.

There are _____ more 🕷 than 🐜.

8 is _____ more than 3.

1   2   3   4   5   6   ⑦   ⑧   ⑨   10

9 is _____ more than 6.

1   2   3   4   5   6   7   8   9   10

6 is _____ more than 2.

1   2   3   4   5   6   7   8   9   10

10 is _____ more than 7.

1   2   3   4   5   6   7   8   9   10

8 is _____ more than 4.

☐ Write the extra numbers to find 4 more.

5 __6__ __7__ __8__ __9__
__9__ is 4 more than 5.

7 ____ ____ ____ ____
____ is 4 more than 7.

4 ____ ____ ____ ____
____ is 4 more than 4.

2 ____ ____ ____ ____
____ is 4 more than 2.

6 ____ ____ ____ ____
____ is 4 more than 6.

9 ____ ____ ____ ____
____ is 4 more than 9.

8 ____ ____ ____ ____
____ is 4 more than 8.

10 ____ ____ ____ ____
____ is 4 more than 10.

3 ____ ____ ____ ____
____ is 4 more than 3.

12 ____ ____ ____ ____
____ is 4 more than 12.

15 ____ ____ ____ ____
_____

11 ____ ____ ____ ____
_____

There are some apples in the bag.

How many apples altogether?

_8_ apples altogether.
_8_ is 3 more than 5.

____ apples altogether.
____ is 4 more than 4.

____ apples altogether.
____ is 3 more than 3.

____ apples altogether.
____ is 4 more than 2.

____ apples altogether.
____ is 4 more than 5.

____ apples altogether.
____ is 1 more than 8.

____ apples altogether.
____ is ____ more than ____.

____ apples altogether.
____ is ____ more than ____.

Reading Number Words to Ten

☐ Match the numbers to the words.

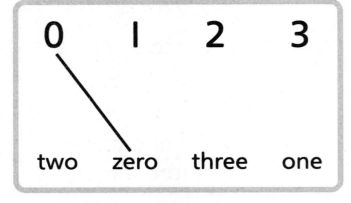

0	1	2	3
two	zero	three	one

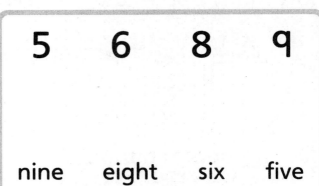

5	6	8	9
nine	eight	six	five

4	7	6	8	3	9
seven	three	four	nine	six	eight

1	4	2	6	5	8
six	one	two	eight	four	five

7	3	9	2	1	4
three	nine	four	seven	two	one

☐ Write the numbers above the number words.

> 8   1
> Eric has eight pencils and one eraser.

Alex is nine years old and Sam is ten years old.

Jane has seven crayons, two markers, and zero pens.

Ronin has five brothers and his sister has six brothers.

Cathy has three sisters and her brother has four sisters.

☐ Write your own sentence with a number word.

Have a friend write the number above the word.

Addition

☐ Add.

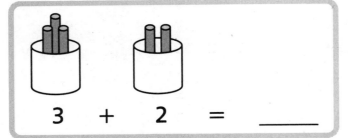

3 + 2 = _____

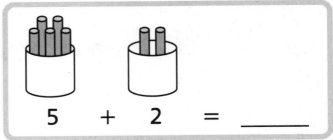

5 + 2 = _____

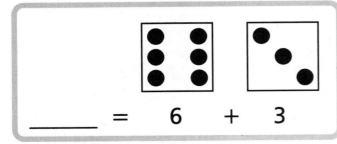

_____ = 6 + 3

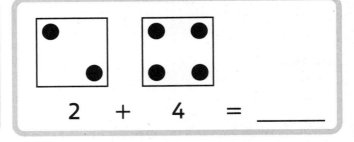

2 + 4 = _____

☐ Write the addition sentence.

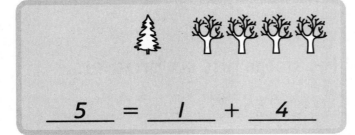

__5__ = __1__ + __4__

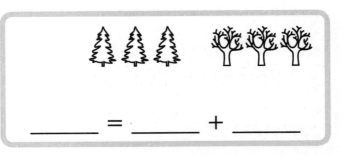

_____ = _____ + _____

_____
+ 6

+ _____

_____ + _____ + _____ = _____

☐ Draw dots to add.

3   +   2   +   4   =   _q_

_____ = 5 + 1 + 4

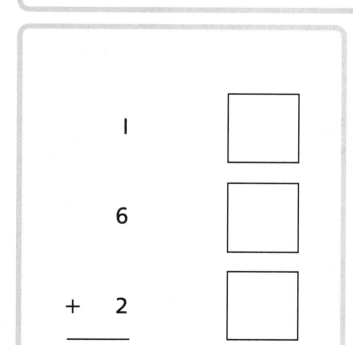

Make your own.

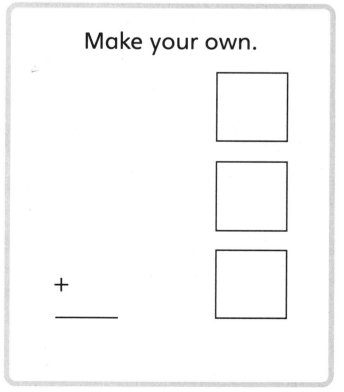

Subtraction

☐ Subtract.

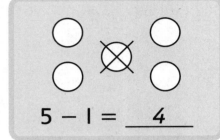

5 − 1 = ___4___

4 − 1 = _____

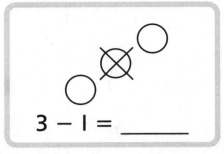

3 − 1 = _____

5 − 2 = _____

4 − 3 = _____

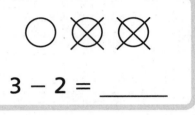

3 − 2 = _____

Braden takes away the black hearts.
How many are left?

3 − 1 = _____

6 − 1 = _____

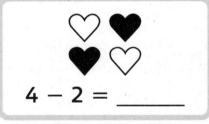

4 − 2 = _____

5 − 3 = _____

5 − 4 = _____

4 − 3 = _____

☐ Write a subtraction sentence for the picture.

☐ Cross out the circles and subtract.

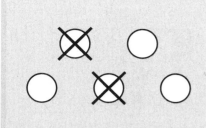

5 − 2 = __3__

○ ○
○ ○

4 − 3 = _____

○
○ ○
○ ○
○

5 − 4 = _____

○ ○ ○
○ ○ ○

6 − 2 = _____

○ ○ ○ ○
○ ○ ○

7 − 4 = _____

☐ Draw a picture to subtract.

4 − 1 = __3__

5 − 3 = _____

4 − 2 = _____

6 − 3 = _____

Make your own.

Adding and Subtracting 0

☐ Add 0 dots.

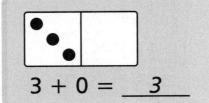

$3 + 0 = \underline{\quad 3 \quad}$

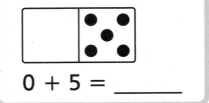

$0 + 5 = \underline{\qquad}$

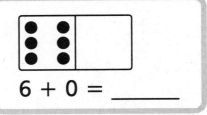

$6 + 0 = \underline{\qquad}$

$0 + 8 = \underline{\qquad}$

$0 + 9 = \underline{\qquad}$

Bonus

$36 + 0 = \underline{\qquad}$

☐ Take away 0 objects.

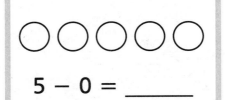

$5 - 0 = \underline{\qquad}$

$7 - 0 = \underline{\qquad}$

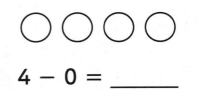

$4 - 0 = \underline{\qquad}$

$8 - 0 = \underline{\qquad}$

$10 - 0 = \underline{\qquad}$

Bonus

$27 - 0 = \underline{\qquad}$

☐ Take away all the objects.

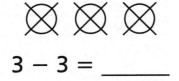

$3 - 3 = \underline{\qquad}$

$5 - 5 = \underline{\qquad}$

$4 - 4 = \underline{\qquad}$

$9 - 9 = \underline{\qquad}$

$8 - 8 = \underline{\qquad}$

Bonus

$99 - 99 = \underline{\qquad}$

📓 What is $7 + 0$? What is $7 - 0$? Explain why.

Counting to 20

Ben has 10 apples.

 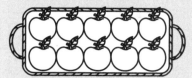

Ben gets more apples.

$10 + \underline{\;1\;} = \underline{\;1\;}\;\underline{\;1\;}$ apples

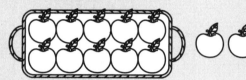

$10 + \underline{\;2\;} = \underline{\;1\;}\;\underline{\;2\;}$ apples

☐ How many apples altogether? Add.

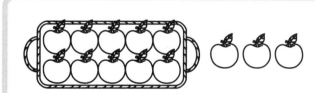

$10 + \underline{\;\;\;} = \underline{\;1\;}\;\underline{\;\;\;}$ apples

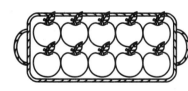

$10 + \underline{\;\;\;} = \underline{\;\;\;}\;\underline{\;\;\;}$ apples

☐ Add.

10	10	10	10	10	10	10	10	10
+ 1	+ 2	+ 3	+ 4	+ 5	+ 6	+ 7	+ 8	+ 9
1 1	__ __	__ __	__ __	__ __	__ __	__ __	__ __	__ __

How many?

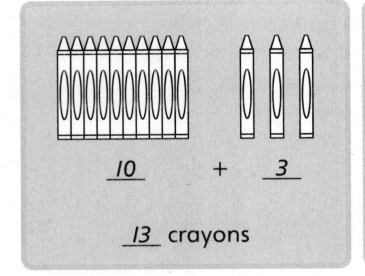

_10_   +   _3_

_13_ crayons

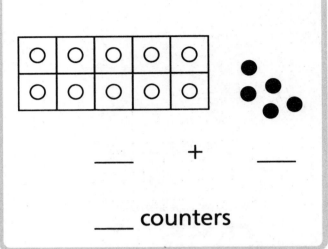

___   +   ___

___ counters

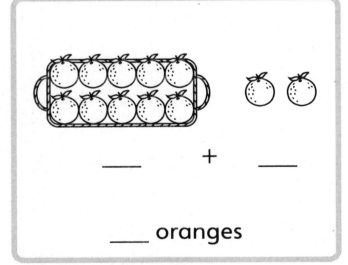

___   +   ___

___ oranges

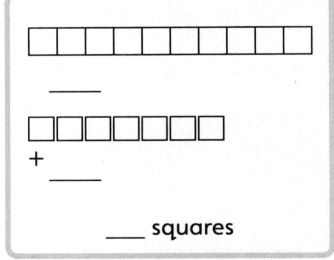

___

+
___

___ squares

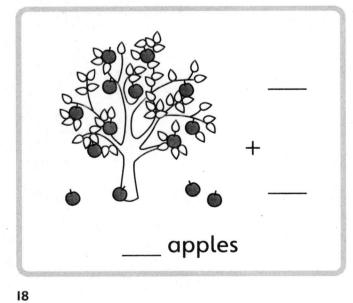

___

+

___

___ apples

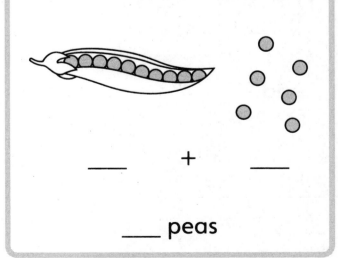

___   +   ___

___ peas

Adding Using a Chart

☐ Circle the next 4 squares.
☐ Add.

| 1 | 2 | 3 | ④ | ⑤ | ⑥ | ⑦ | 8 | 9 | 10 |

3 + 4 = __7__

| 1 | 2 | 3 | 4 | 5 | 6 | 7 | 8 | 9 | 10 |

2 + 4 = ____

| 1 | 2 | 3 | 4 | 5 | 6 | 7 | 8 | 9 | 10 |

6 + 4 = ____

| 1 | 2 | 3 | 4 | 5 | 6 | 7 | 8 | 9 | 10 |
| 11 | 12 | 13 | 14 | 15 | 16 | 17 | 18 | 19 | 20 |

9 + 4 = ____

| 1 | 2 | 3 | 4 | 5 | 6 | 7 | 8 | 9 | 10 |
| 11 | 12 | 13 | 14 | 15 | 16 | 17 | 18 | 19 | 20 |

8 + 4 = ____

☐ Shade the first number of squares.
☐ Circle the second number of squares.
☐ Add.

1	2	3	4	5	6	7	⑧	⑨	⑩
⑪	⑫	⑬	14	15	16	17	18	19	20

7 + 6 = __13__

1	2	3	4	5	6	7	8	9	10
11	12	13	14	15	16	17	18	19	20

6 + 9 = _____

1	2	3	4	5	6	7	8	9	10
11	12	13	14	15	16	17	18	19	20

8 + 8 = _____

1	2	3	4	5	6	7	8	9	10
11	12	13	14	15	16	17	18	19	20

7 + 9 = _____

1	2	3	4	5	6	7	8	9	10
11	12	13	14	15	16	17	18	19	20

9 + 4 = _____

Tina pretends the first number of squares are shaded.
Then she circles the second number of squares.

| 1 | 2 | 3 | 4 | ⑤ | ⑥ | ⑦ | 8 | 9 | 10 |

$4 + 3 = \underline{7}$

☐ Use Tina's way to add.

| 1 | 2 | 3 | 4 | 5 | ⑥ | ⑦ | 8 | 9 | 10 |

$5 + 2 = \underline{}$

| 1 | 2 | 3 | ④ | ⑤ | ⑥ | ⑦ | ⑧ | ⑨ | 10 |

$3 + 6 = \underline{}$

| 1 | 2 | 3 | 4 | 5 | 6 | 7 | 8 | 9 | 10 |

$4 + 2 = \underline{}$

| 1 | 2 | 3 | 4 | 5 | 6 | 7 | 8 | 9 | 10 |

$5 + 3 = \underline{}$

| 1 | 2 | 3 | 4 | 5 | 6 | 7 | 8 | 9 | 10 |
| 11 | 12 | 13 | 14 | 15 | 16 | 17 | 18 | 19 | 20 |

$7 + 5 = \underline{}$

☐ Add.

1	2	3	4	5
6	7	8	9	10

5 + 3 = ____

1	2	3	4	5
6	7	8	9	10

6 + 2 = ____

1	2	3	4	5
6	7	8	9	10

3 + 5 = ____

1	2	3	4	5
6	7	8	9	10

2 + 6 = ____

1	2	3	4	5	6	7	8	9	10
11	12	13	14	15	16	17	18	19	20

5 + 9 = ____

1	2	3	4	5	6	7	8	9	10
11	12	13	14	15	16	17	18	19	20

9 + 5 = ____

What do you notice? _____

_____

Tens and Ones Blocks

One row of 10 and how many more ones?

1	2	3	4	5	6	7	8	9	10
11	12	13	14	15	16	17	18	19	20

13 =

1 row of 10 + ____ more ones

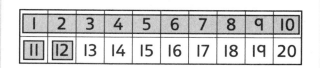

12 =

1 row of 10 + ____ more ones

19 =

1 row of 10 + ____ more ones

16 =

1 row of 10 + ____ more ones

17 =

1 row of 10 + ____ more ones

18 =

1 row of 10 + ____ more ones

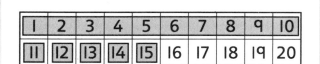

15 =

1 row of 10 + ____ more ones

14 =

1 row of 10 + ____ more ones

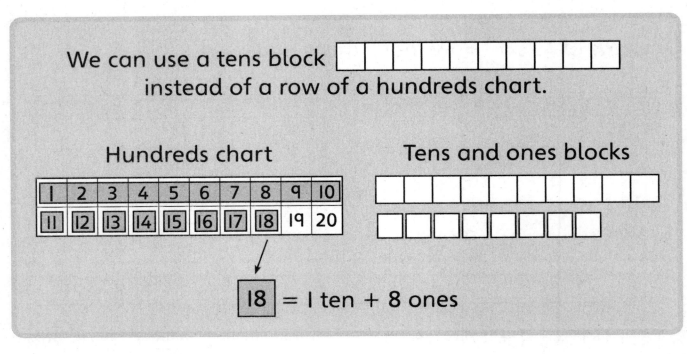

We can use a tens block instead of a row of a hundreds chart.

Hundreds chart

1	2	3	4	5	6	7	8	9	10
11	12	13	14	15	16	17	18	19	20

Tens and ones blocks

18 = 1 ten + 8 ones

What number do the blocks show?

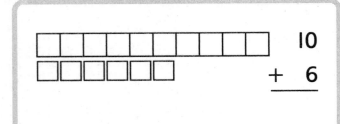
10
+ 6

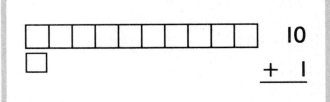
10
+ 1

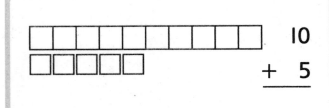
10
+ 5

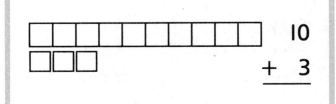
10
+ 3

10
+ 9

10
+ 7

Reading Number Words to Twenty

☐ Underline the beginning letters that are the same.

<u>six</u>　　　<u>six</u>teen	two　　　twelve
three　　　thirteen	four　　　fourteen
eight　　　eighteen	five　　　fifteen

☐ Circle the digits that are the same.

②　　　1②	6　　　16	7　　　17
9　　　19	8　　　18	3　　　13

☐ Underline and circle the same parts.

<u>three</u> = ③ <u>thir</u>teen = 1③	four = 4 fourteen = 14
five = 5 fifteen = 15	nine = 9 nineteen = 19
seven = 7 seventeen = 17	two = 2 twelve = 12

☐ Write the number.

thirteen = _1_ _3_   **seven**teen = __ __   **fif**teen = __ __

sixteen = __ __   fourteen = __ __   twelve = __ __

nineteen = __ __   eighteen = __ __   eleven = __ __

☐ Match the word with the number.

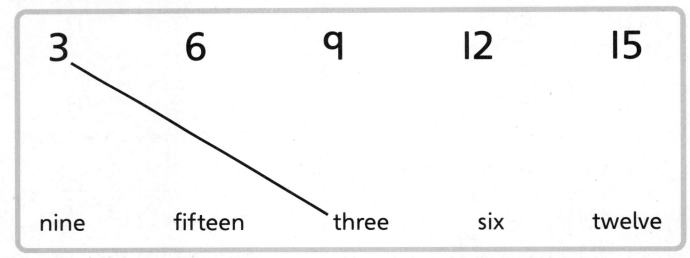

3   6   9   12   15

nine   fifteen   three   six   twelve

11   13   15   17   19

fifteen   nineteen   thirteen   eleven   seventeen

☐ Write the number above the number word.

| 13 |
| Ella is thirteen months old. |

Marcel has twenty teeth.

Sixteen friends played tag.

Holidays start in eleven days.

We played basketball for fifteen minutes.

Cody invited eighteen friends to his birthday party.

Bonus

Amy's soccer team has twelve players —

seven girls and five boys.

☐ Write your own sentence with a number word.

Have a partner write the number above the word.

Writing Number Words to Twenty

☐ Answer the question using both the number and the word.

What grade are you in? _2_ = __two__

How many letters are in your first name? ____ = _____

How old are you? ____ = _____

How many pets do you have? ____ = _____

How many children are in your class? ____ = _____

How many weeks are in a year? ____ = _____

How many months are in a year? ____ = _____

How many blank lines (_) are on this page? ____ = _____

Bonus

How many letters are always consonants? ____ = _____

a **b** **c** **d** e **f** **g** **h** i **j** **k** **l** **m** **n** o **p** **q** **r** **s** **t** u **v** **w** **x** y **z**

First Word Problems

Add using the pictures.

1 car   2 more cars

1 + 2 = _____

2 cars   3 more cars

2 + 3 = _____

5 cars   3 more cars

5 + 3 = _____

2 cars   6 more cars

2 + 6 = _____

☐ Write the numbers above the number words.
☐ Draw counters to show the numbers.
☐ Write the number sentence.
☐ Write the answer as a word.

                    3
There are three cats.   ○ ○ ○

                    4
There are four dogs.   ○ ○ ○ ○

                                    3
                                +   4
                                    ‾‾‾
There are ___seven___ animals altogether.   7

There are six yellow crayons.

There are five blue crayons.

There are _____ crayons in total.

                                ☐
                            +   ☐
                                ‾‾‾
                                ☐

There are two big toys.

There are eight small toys.

There are _____ toys in total.

                                ☐
                            +   ☐
                                ‾‾‾
                                ☐

Alice has seven shirts.

John has six shirts.

They have _____ shirts altogether.

                                ☐
                            +   ☐
                                ‾‾‾
                                ☐

- ☐ Write the numbers above the number words.
- ☐ Draw circles and cross some out to subtract.
- ☐ Write the subtraction sentence.
- ☐ Write the answer as a word.

8
Jack had eight crayons. ⊗⊗⊗○○○○○   8
3
He gave three to his sister. − 3

Jack has ____five____ crayons left.   5

Glen had four pencils.

He lost one of them.   −

Glen has _____ pencils left.

Lily had six marbles.

She gave two to Kate.   −

Lily has _____ marbles left.

Simon had five toy cars.

His teacher took three of them.   −

Now Simon has _____ toy cars.

Making Word Problems

What are you adding together?

3 big frogs

2 small frogs

_____ *frogs*

2 red marbles

4 green marbles

_____

3 new pencils

5 used pencils

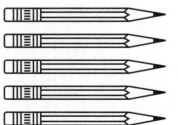

_____

4 big paperclips

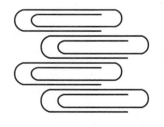

7 small paperclips

_____

6 red apples

6 green apples

_____

☐ Add.
☐ Write what you are adding.

There are 5 big frogs.

There are 2 small frogs.

There are __7__ ___frogs___ altogether.

There are 4 new pencils.

There are 2 used pencils.

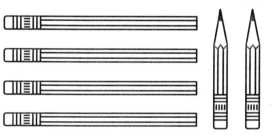

There are ___ _____ altogether.

There are 5 red apples.

There are 5 green apples.

There are ___ _____ altogether.

There are 3 empty cups.

There are 2 full cups.

There are ___ _____ altogether.

☐ Use the words to make a problem for each picture.

~~big~~   ~~small~~   empty   full
farm   zoo   happy   sad

There are __3__ ___*big*___ frogs.
There are __2__ ___*small*___ frogs.

There are __5__ frogs altogether.

There are ___ _____ bowls.
There are ___ _____ bowls.

There are __5__ bowls altogether.

There are ___ _____ animals.
There are ___ _____ animals.

There are ___ animals altogether.

There are ___ _____ faces.
There are ___ _____ faces.

There are ___ faces altogether.

☐ Write a question that matches Rani's answer.
☐ Finish her answer.

Question: _____ *There are 3 big bears.* _____

_____ *There are 2 small bears.* _____

_____ *How many bears altogether?* _____

Answer:

There are 5 bears altogether.

$$\underline{\;3\;} + \underline{\;2\;} = \underline{\;5\;}$$

Question: _____

_____

_____

Answer:

There are 9 faces altogether.

$$\underline{\quad} + \underline{\quad} = \underline{\quad}$$

☐ Write a problem for the picture.
☐ Write the subtraction sentence.

There are 10 flies.

The frog eats 3 of them.

How many are left?

$\underline{10} - \underline{3} = \underline{7}$

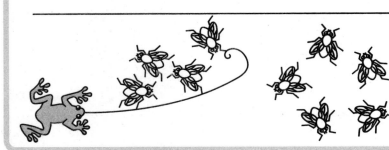

___ − ___ = ___

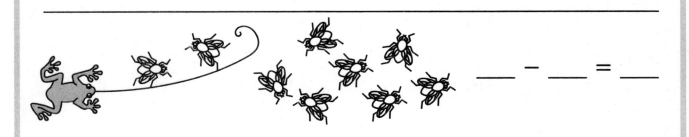

___ − ___ = ___

☐ Write a problem for the picture.
☐ Write the subtraction sentence.

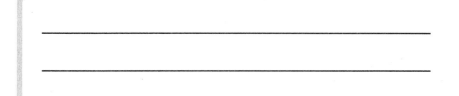

There were 9 apples in the tree.

4 of them fell.

How many are left?

___ – ___ = ___

_____

_____

_____

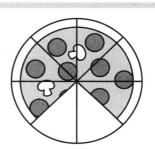

___ – ___ = ___

_____

_____

_____

___ – ___ = ___

Cores of Patterns

The parts that repeat are the **core**.
Each part is a **term**.

☐ Circle the core.

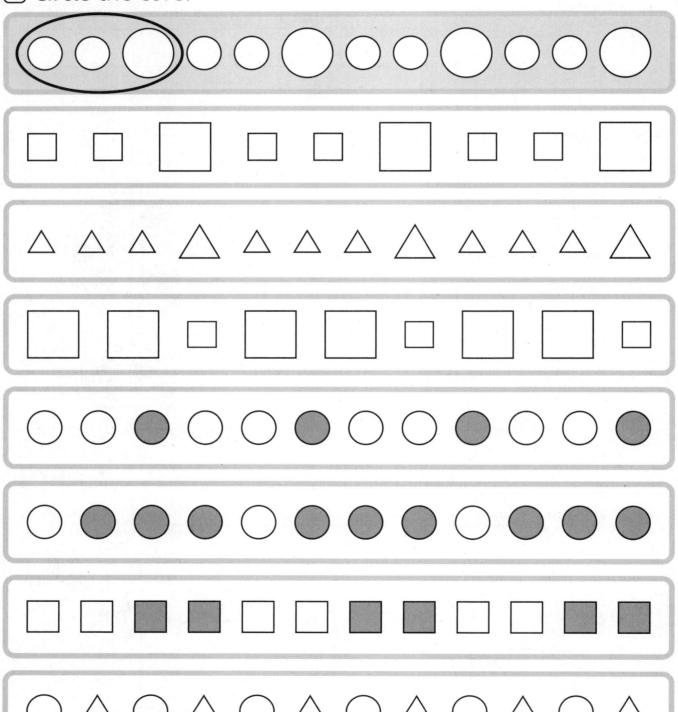

Patterns and Algebra 2-1

☐ Circle the core.
☐ Draw the next three terms.

○ ○ ○ ◯ ○ ○ ○ ◯ ○ ○ ○ ◯   ○ ○ ○ ___ ___ ___

□ □ ◻ □ □ ◻ □ □ ◻ ___ ___ ___

□ △ ○ □ △ ○ □ △ ○ ___ ___ ___

1 7 7 1 7 7 1 7 7 ___ ___ ___

□ □ □ ○ ○ □ □ □ ○ ○ □ □ □ ___ ___ ___

1 2 3 3 1 2 3 3 1 2 ___ ___ ___

A A ∀ A A ∀ ___ ___ ___

___ ___ ___

What Changes?

Which **attribute** changes?

3 Ɛ 3 Ɛ size (direction)	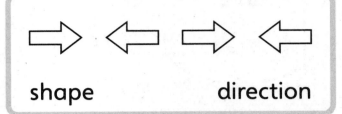 shape direction

b c b c b c

shape   direction

b d b d b d

colour   direction

size   colour   shape

B B B B B B B B B B B B

direction   shape   size   colour

B B Ɓ B B Ɓ B B Ɓ

direction   colour   size   thickness

B **B** B **B** B **B** B **B**

direction   shape   size   thickness

     Patterns and Algebra 2-2

☐ What changes? Choose **two**.

direction   size   shape   colour   thickness

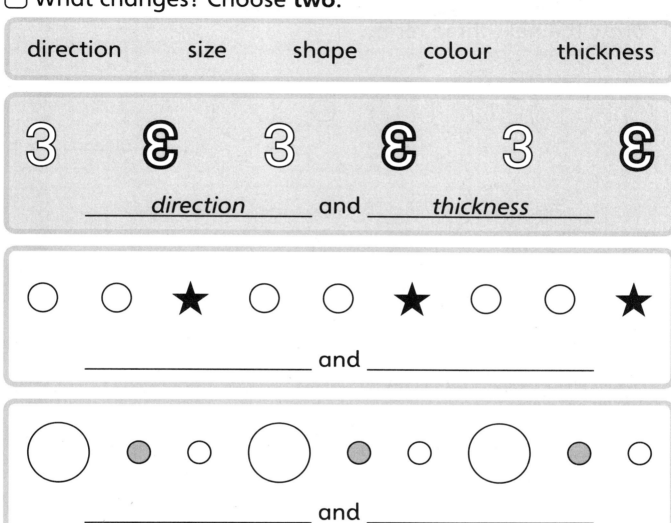

direction _____ and _____ thickness _____

_____ and _____

_____ and _____

_____ and _____

_____ and _____

☐ Circle the core.
☐ Draw the next three terms.

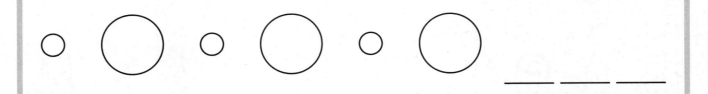

____ ____ ____

____ ____ ____

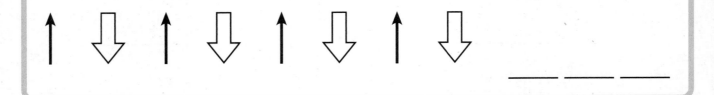

____ ____ ____

↑ ⇓ ↑ ⇓ ↑ ⇓ ↑ ⇓

____ ____ ____

2 2 **2** **2** 2 **2**

____ ____ ____

A A B A A B

____ ____ ____

Patterns and Algebra 2-2

☐ Create a pattern.

only **colour** changes

○ ○ ○ ○ ○ ○ ○ ○ ○

only **size** changes

only **shape** changes

colour and **size** change

colour and **shape** change

☐ Create a pattern where 2 attributes change. What changes?

Pattern Rules

☐ Circle the core.
☐ Describe how the attribute changes. Choose two.

thin	thick	small	big	light	dark

_____thin_____ , _____thick_____ , _____repeat_____

_____ , _____ , _____ , _____repeat_____

_____ , _____ , _____ , _____repeat_____

_____ , _____ , _____ , _____ , _____repeat_____

☐ Now say when to repeat as well.

_____

Patterns and Algebra 2-3

☐ Describe how **two** attributes change.

Size: ___*big*___, ___*small*___, ___*small*___, ___*repeat*___

Direction: ___*up*___, _____, _____, _____

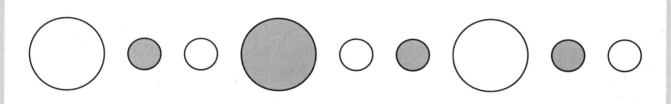

Size: _____, _____, _____, ___*repeat*___

Colour: _____, _____, _____

Shape: _____, _____, _____, ___*repeat*___

Thickness: _____, _____, _____, _____

☐ Describe the pattern.

big   small   circle   triangle

_____circle_____, _____, _____repeat_____

_____big_____, _____, _____, _____repeat_____

up   down   dark   light

_____dark_____, _____, _____, _____, _____

_____, _____, _____

thin   thick   big   small

_____thick_____, _____, _____, _____

_____, _____, _____, _____, _____

Patterns and Algebra 2-3

Showing Patterns in Different Ways

☐ Use letters to show the pattern.
   Put the same letter under the same figures.

A B B A B B

__ __ __ __ __ __

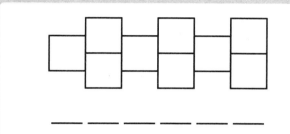

__ __ __ __ __ __

7 0 9 7 0 9

__ __ __ __ __ __

| | — — | |

__ __ __ __ __ __

+ ✓ — ✓ + ✓

__ __ __ __ __ __

__ __ __ __ __ __

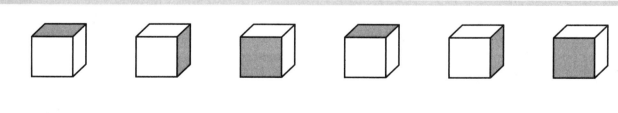

__ __ __ __ __ __ __ __ __ __ __ __

☐ Show the pattern in two ways. Use ☺, ☹, 😐, and numbers.

A	B	B	A	B	B	A	B	B
☺	☹	☹	☺	☹	☹	☺	☹	☹
1	2	2	1	2	2	1	2	2

A	B	C	A	B	C	A	B	C
☺	☹	😐	☺	○	○	○	○	○
7	8	9	7	___	___	___	___	___

A	B	C	C	A	B	C	C	A	B	C	C
○	○	○	○	○	○	○	○	○	○	○	○

___ ___ ___ ___ ___ ___ ___ ___ ___ ___ ___ ___

△	□	□	◇	△	□	□	◇	△	□	□	◇
○	○	○	○	○	○	○	○	○	○	○	○

___ ___ ___ ___ ___ ___ ___ ___ ___ ___ ___ ___

Patterns and Algebra 2-4

Length

☐ Colour the **longer** pencil.

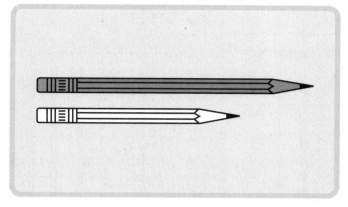

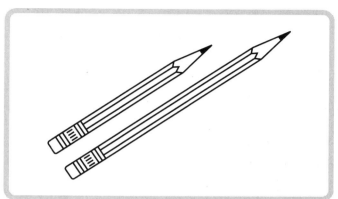

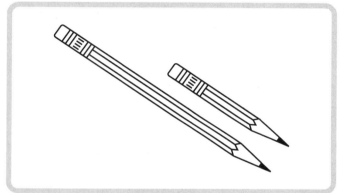

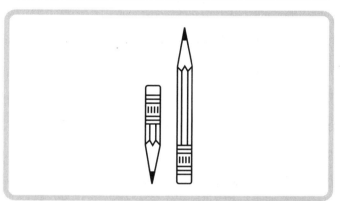

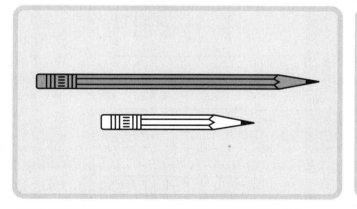

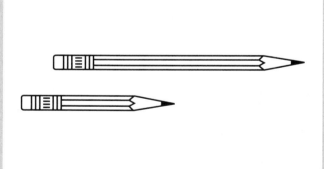

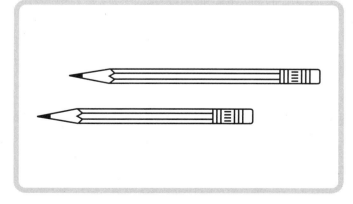

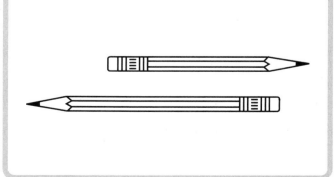

☐ Cut 4 strips of paper. Is the top **longer** or **shorter** than the side? Use the strips to compare.

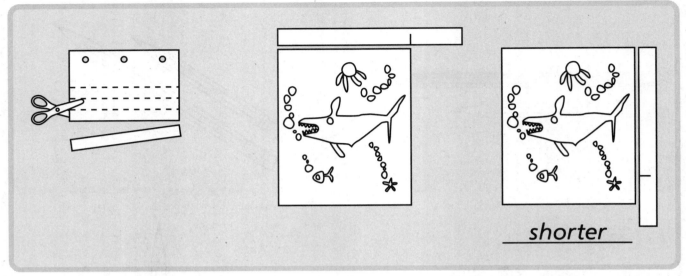

shorter

_____

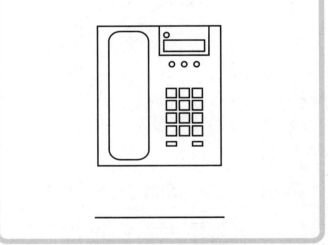

_____

_____

_____

Width, Height, and Distance Around

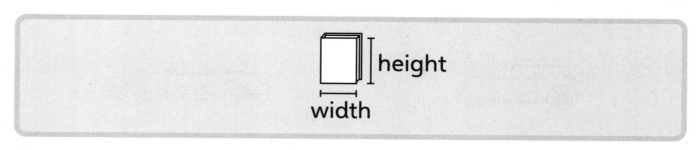

height

width

☐ Colour the line showing **width** blue.
☐ Colour the line showing **height** red.

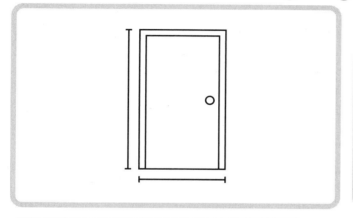

CEREAL

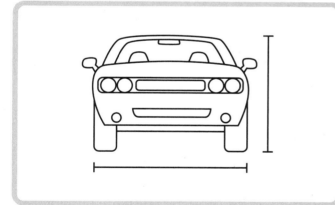

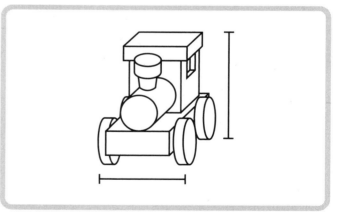

Bonus

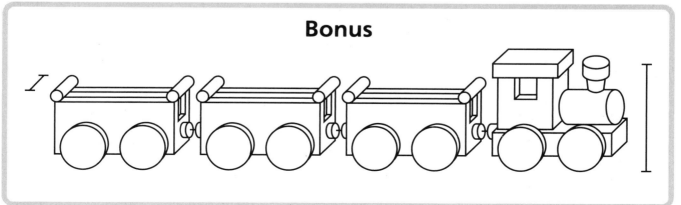

☐ Write **long** or **short**.

This car is ___*short*___.

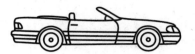

This car is _____.

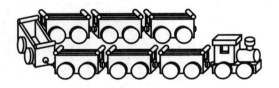

This train is _____.

This train is _____.

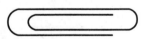

This paper clip is _____.

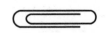

This paper clip is _____.

This pencil is _____.

This pencil is _____.

☐ Which is **longer**?

The long car or the short train. _____

The long paper clip or the short pencil. _____

Measurement 2-2

☐ Name the children.

Billy says Marko is tall.
Sam says Marko is short.

_____   _____   _____

Rob says Jax has short hair.
Rob says Tom has long hair.

_____   _____   _____

Bonus
Tessa says Mary has short hair.
Rani says Sharon has short hair.
Tessa says Sharon has long hair.

_____   _____   _____   _____

☐ Cut a string to match the distance around.
☐ Label the string.

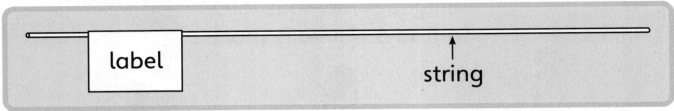

label

string

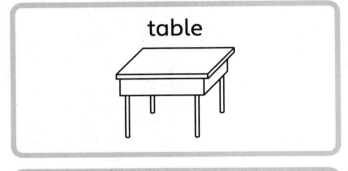

table

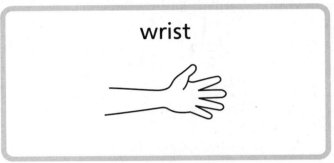

wrist

mug

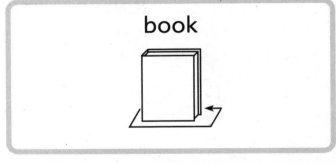

book

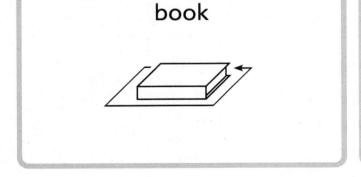

book

your choice

☐ Order the objects from longest to shortest around.

1. _____   4. _____

2. _____   5. _____

3. _____   6. _____

Measuring Length

Use big 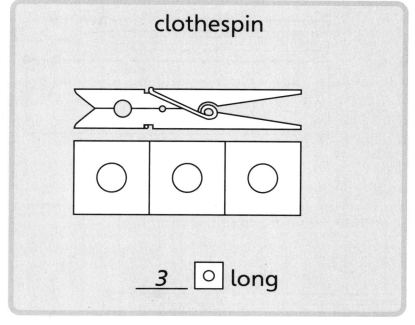.

How many long?

<table>
<tr><td>

clothespin

__3__ ⬚ long

</td><td>

needle

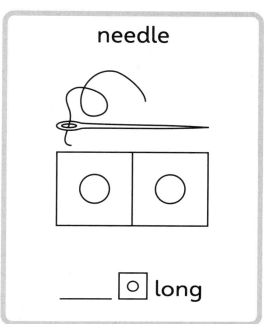

____ ⬚ long

</td></tr>
<tr><td>

worm

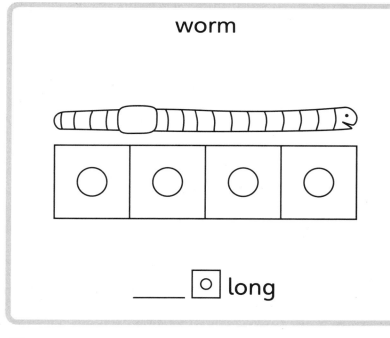

____ ⬚ long

</td><td>

ant

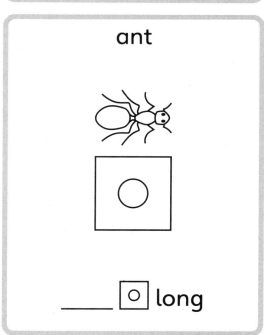

____ ⬚ long

</td></tr>
</table>

☐ Order the needle, ant, and worm from shortest to longest.

_____   _____   _____

shortest   longest

☐ What is the length closer to?

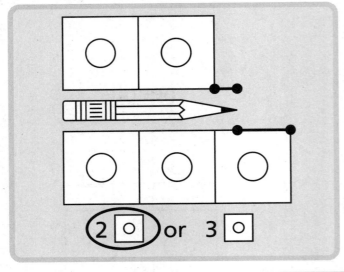

2 ⬚ or 3 ⬚

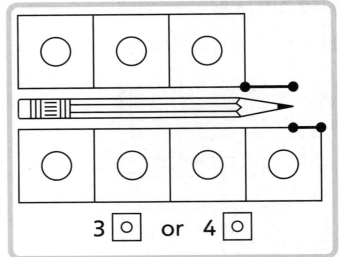

3 ⬚ or 4 ⬚

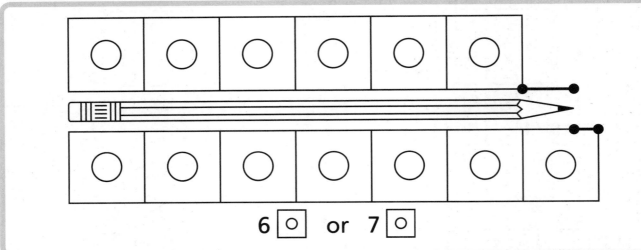

6 ⬚ or 7 ⬚

☐ Measure with big ⬚.

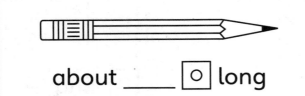

about ____ ⬚ long

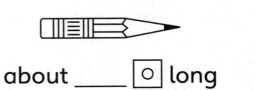

about ____ ⬚ long

about ____ ⬚ long

Units

☐ Circle what you would use to measure the length.
☐ Explain your choice.

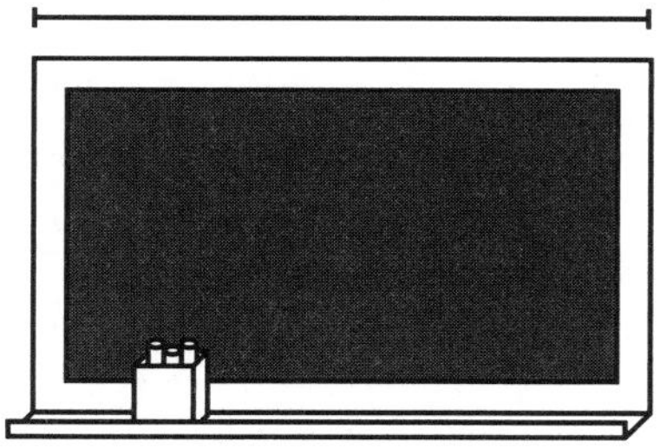

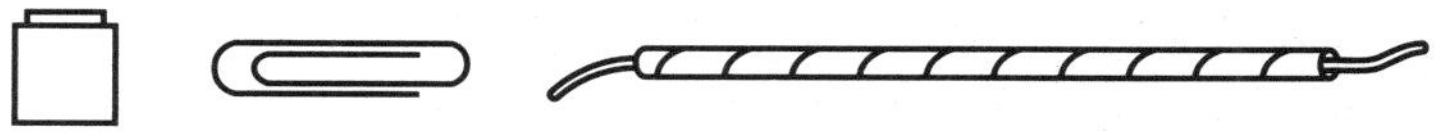

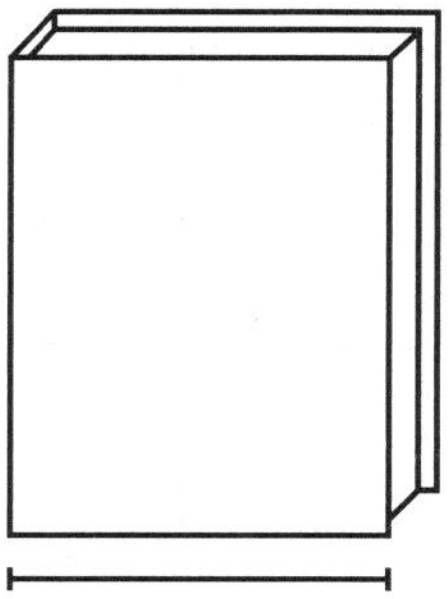

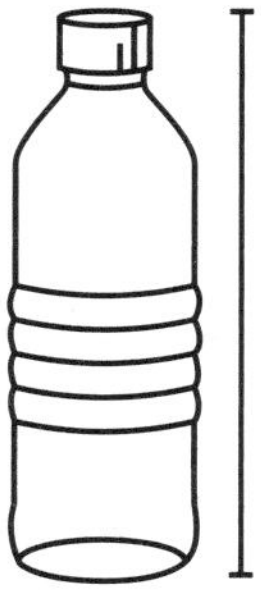

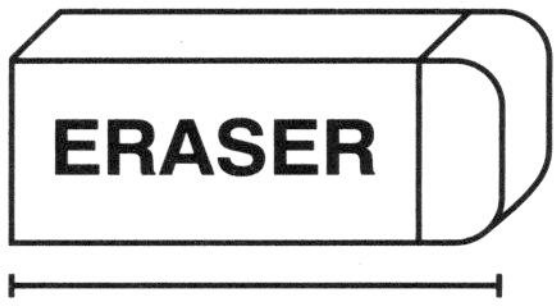

_____

_____

_____

_____

_____

_____

_____

_____

How to Measure

☐ Explain what is wrong with the measurement.

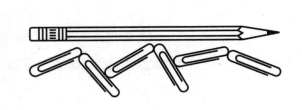

6 ⬭ long

_____

_____

_____

_____

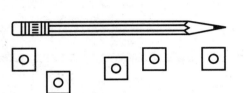

5 ◻ long

_____

_____

_____

_____

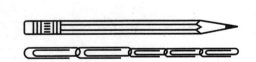

5 ⬭ long

_____

_____

_____

_____

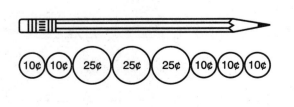

8 coins long

_____

_____

_____

_____

Measuring Distance

☐ How far is the mouse from the cheese? Use big 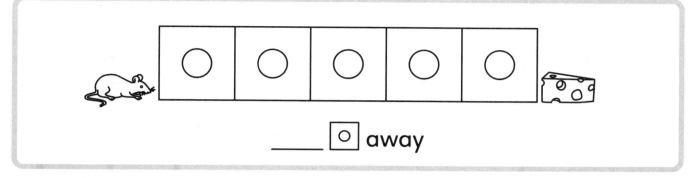.
☐ Circle the mouse that is the farthest from the cheese.

_____ 🔲 away

_____ 🔲 away   _____ 🔲 away   _____ 🔲 away

How long is the path from the mouse to the cheese?

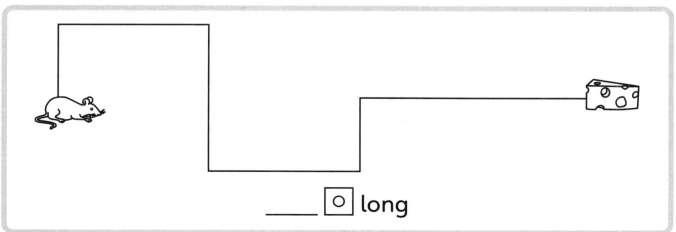

_____ 🔲 long

Measuring the Distance Around

Use small 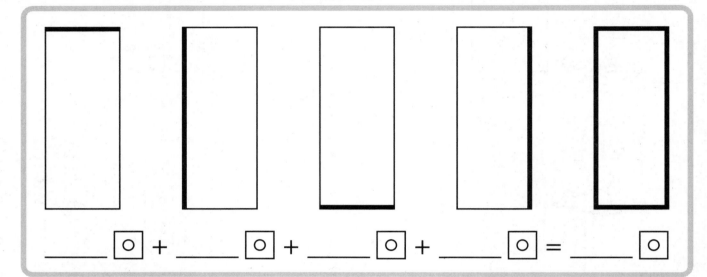.

☐ Find each side length.
☐ Add to find the distance around.

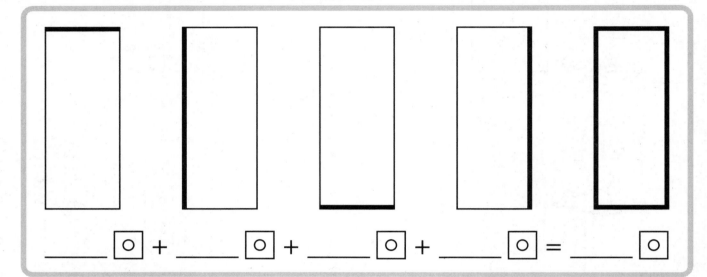

____ 🔘 + ____ 🔘 + ____ 🔘 + ____ 🔘 = ____ 🔘

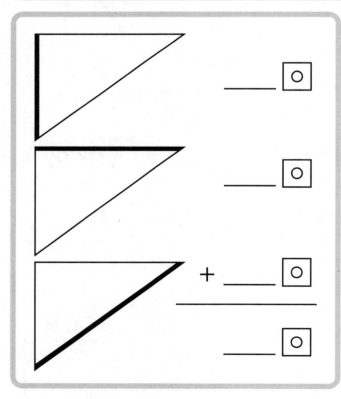

____ 🔘

____ 🔘

+ ____ 🔘

____ 🔘

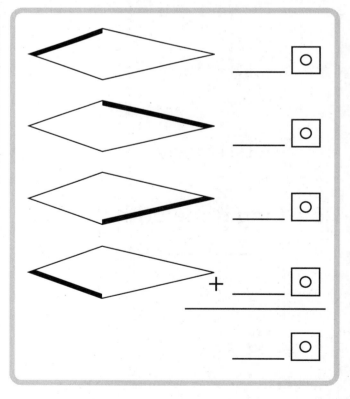

____ 🔘

____ 🔘

____ 🔘

+ ____ 🔘

____ 🔘

☐ Order the distances around. _____ _____ _____

smallest   largest

☐ Use big 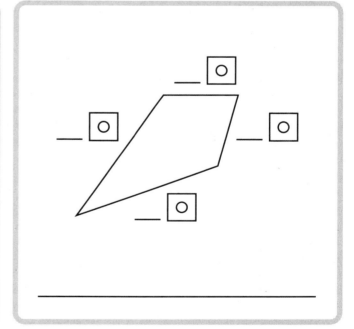 to find each side length.
☐ Write an addition sentence to show the distance around.

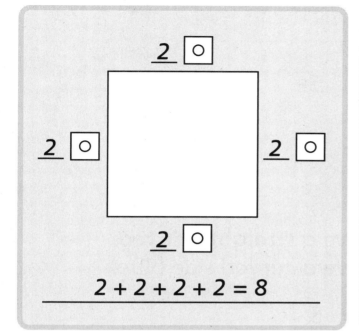

$\underline{2}$ ⬚

$\underline{2}$ ⬚ $\underline{2}$ ⬚

$\underline{2}$ ⬚

$$2 + 2 + 2 + 2 = 8$$
_____

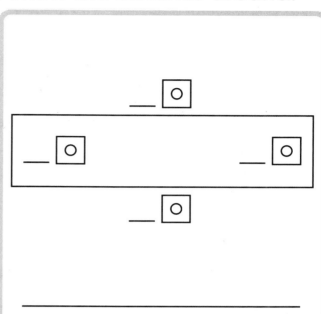

___ ⬚

___ ⬚   ___ ⬚

___ ⬚

_____

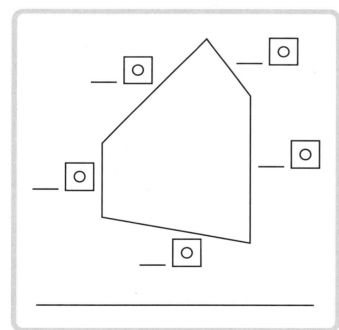

_____

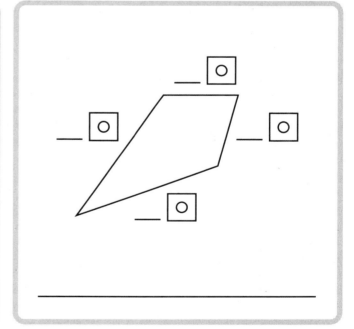

_____

☐ What shape has the **largest** distance around? Colour it blue.
☐ What shape has the **smallest** distance around? Colour it red.
☐ What two shapes have **the same** distance around?
　 Colour them yellow.

Lines

straight lines

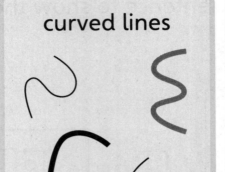
curved lines

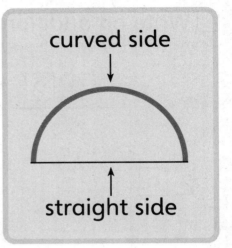
curved side
straight side

☐ Colour all the shapes that have a **straight** side red.
☐ Colour all the shapes that have a **curved** side blue.

red	red blue	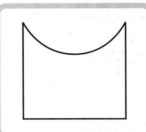	
	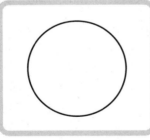	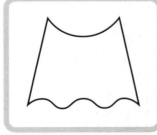	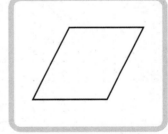
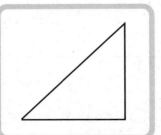			

☐ Fill in the boxes that have purple shapes.
What letter do you see? ____

open lines	closed lines
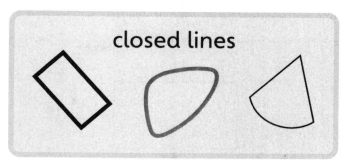	

☐ Put an ✗ on the open lines.
☐ Circle the closed lines.

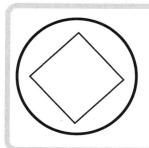 

 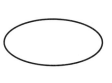

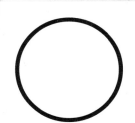  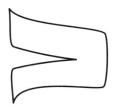

Geometry 2-I

Sides and Vertices

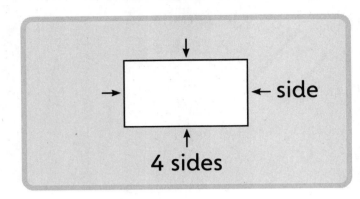

4 sides

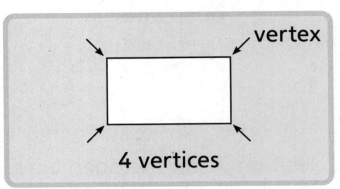

4 vertices

☐ Count the sides.

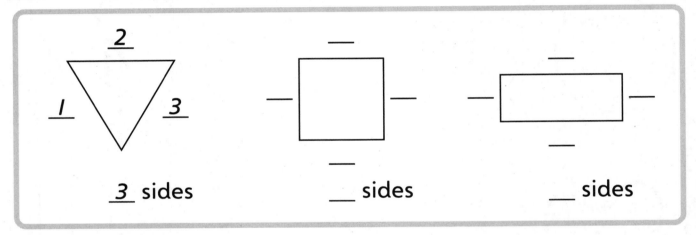

3 sides   __ sides   __ sides

☐ Count the vertices.

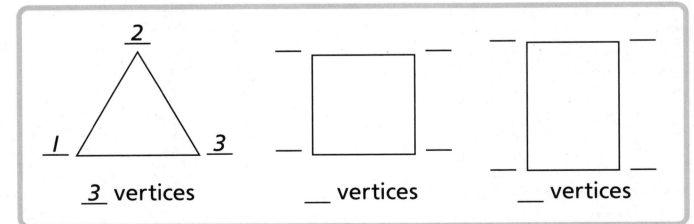

3 vertices   __ vertices   __ vertices

How many sides? ____ How many vertices? ____

☐ ✓ what is true and ✗ what is not true.

☑ 4 sides
☑ 4 vertices

☐ 4 sides
☐ 4 vertices

☐ 4 sides
☐ 4 vertices

☐ 4 sides
☐ 4 vertices

☐ 4 sides
☐ 4 vertices

☐ 4 sides
☐ 4 vertices

☐ 3 sides
☐ 3 vertices
☐ closed line

☐ 3 sides
☐ 3 vertices
☐ closed line

☐ 4 sides
☐ 4 vertices
☐ closed line

☐ 4 sides
☐ 4 vertices
☐ closed line

☐ 3 sides
☐ 3 vertices
☐ straight sides

☐ 4 sides
☐ 4 vertices
☐ straight sides

Squares

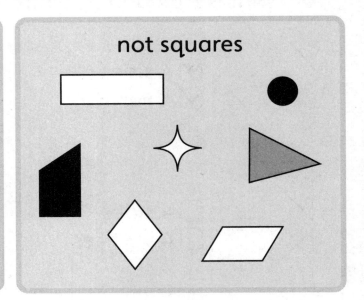

squares	not squares

☐ Put an ✗ on the shapes that are **not** squares.

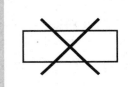

Rectangles

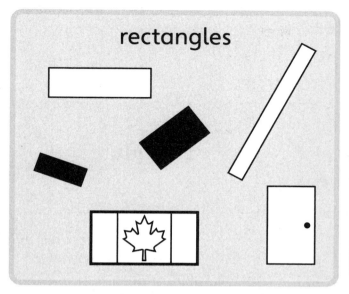

rectangles

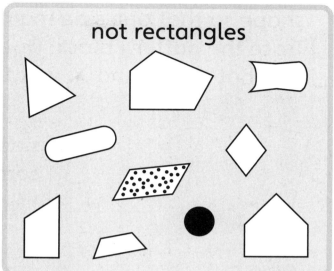

not rectangles

☐ Circle the rectangles.

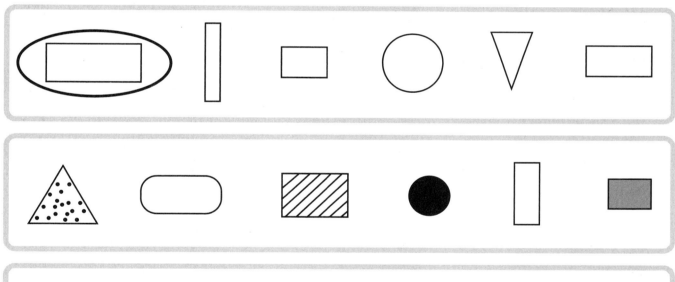

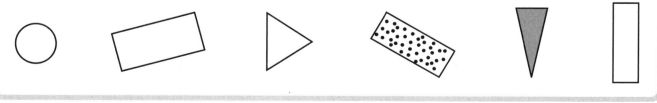

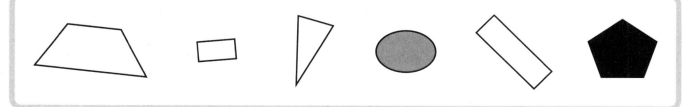

☐ Place a pattern block square on the
   shape so that one side matches.
☐ Trace the pattern block. Does it match?
☐ ✓ what is true and ✗ what is not true.

☐ 4 sides   ☐ square
☐ 4 corners
☐ all sides equal

☐ 4 sides   ☐ square
☐ 4 corners   ☐ rectangle
☐ all sides equal

☐ 4 sides   ☐ square
☐ 4 corners   ☐ rectangle
☐ all sides equal

☐ Draw.

square

rectangle

Triangles

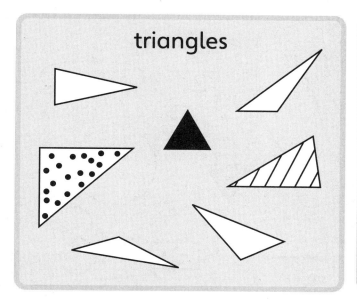

triangles

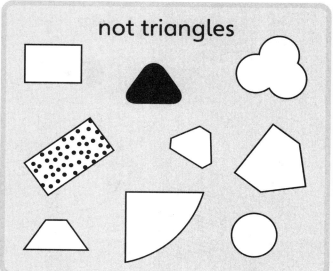

not triangles

☐ Circle the triangles.

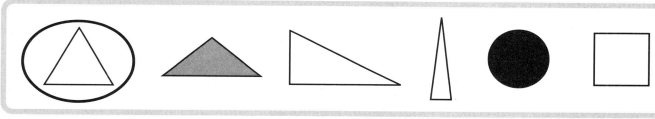

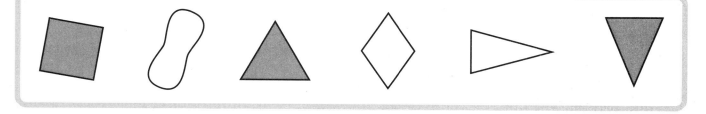

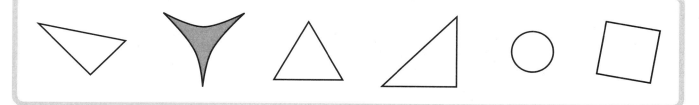

Circles

circles	not circles

☐ Put an ✗ on the shapes that are **not** circles.

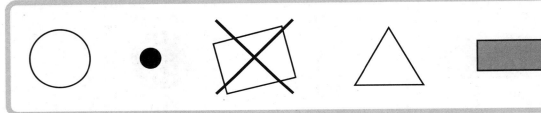

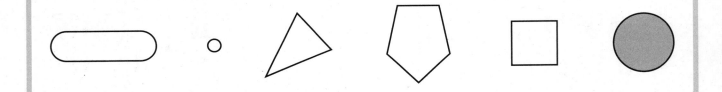

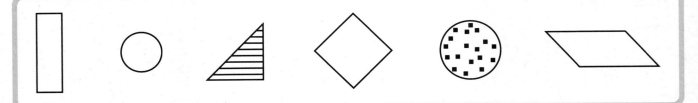

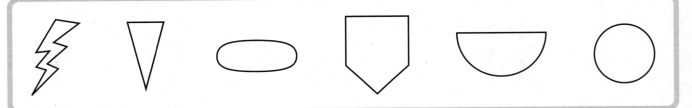

Sorting into Groups

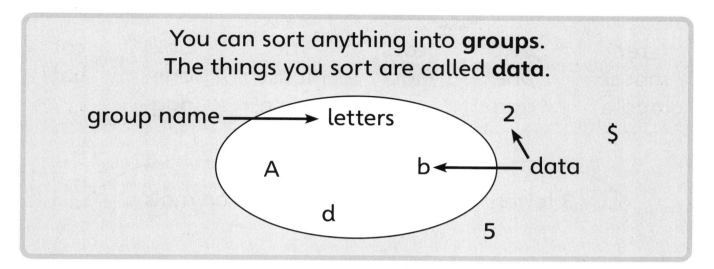

You can sort anything into **groups**.
The things you sort are called **data**.

group name → letters

2

$

A   b ← data

d

5

☐ Sort the data.

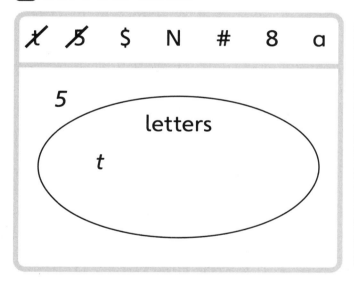

✗ ✗ $ N # 8 a

5

letters

t

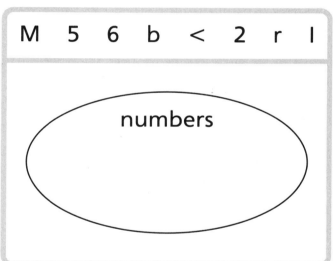

M 5 6 b < 2 r l

numbers

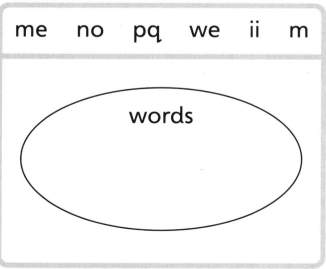

me no pq we ii m

words

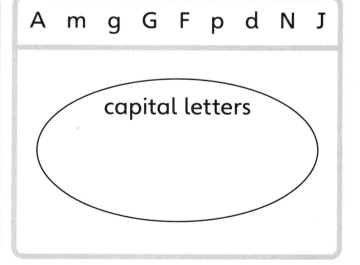

A m g G F p d N J

capital letters

☐ Sort the data.

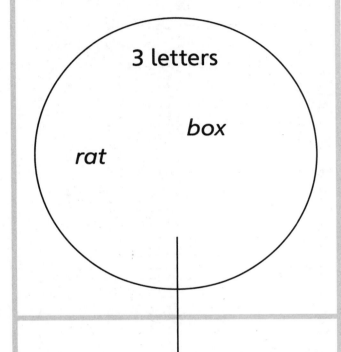

rat box cat
mouse one hat
apple dog

~~rat~~ ~~box~~ cat
mouse one hat
apple dog

3 letters

box

rat

box

animals
with 3 letters

rat

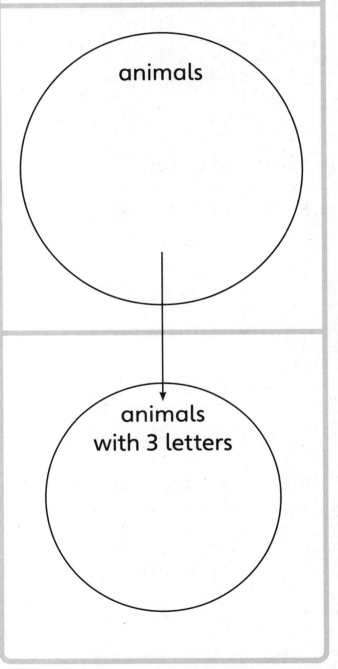

rat box cat
mouse one hat
apple dog

animals

animals
with 3 letters

☐ Did you get the same answer? _____

Probability and Data Management 2-1

☐ Sort the data. Use arrows.

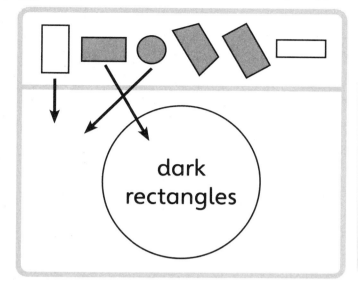

dark rectangles

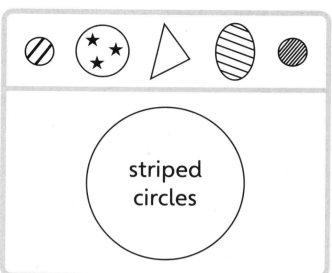

striped circles

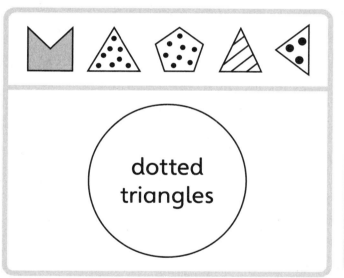

dotted triangles

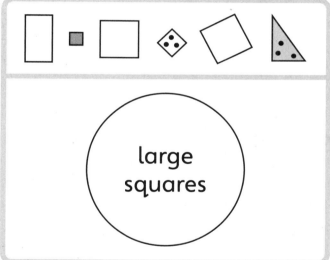

large squares

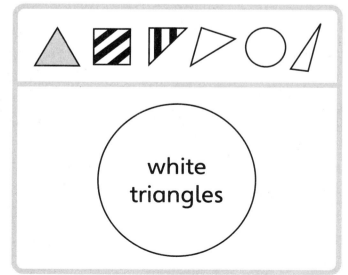

white triangles

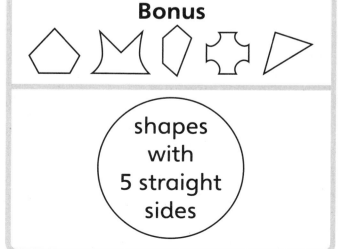

Bonus

shapes with 5 straight sides

Sorting into Many Groups

☐ Sort the data. Use arrows.

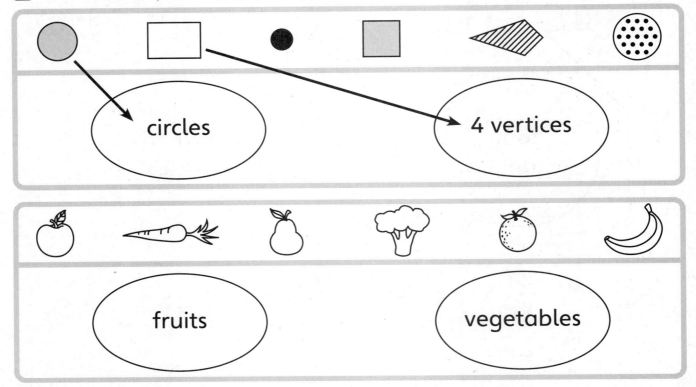

Some objects do not belong in any group.

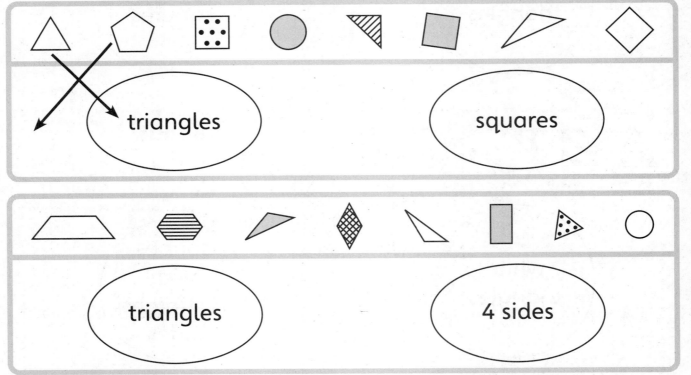

☐ Sort the data. Use arrows.

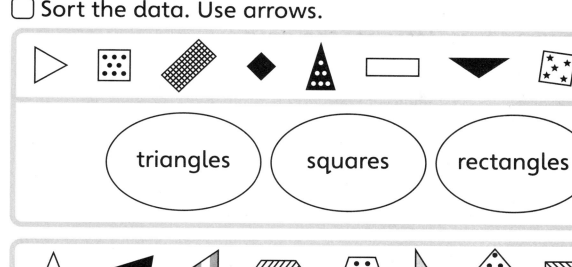

triangles   squares   rectangles

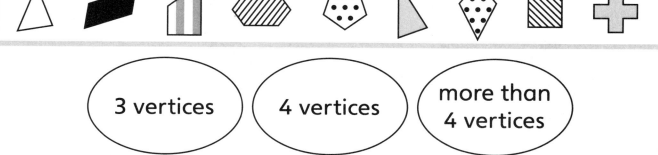

3 vertices   4 vertices   more than 4 vertices

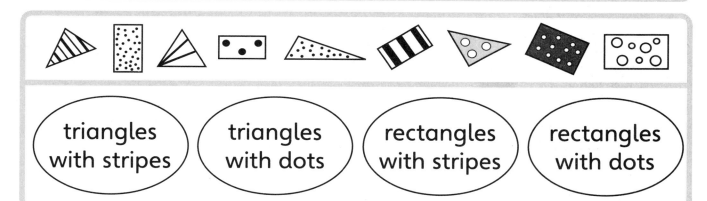

triangles with stripes   triangles with dots   rectangles with stripes   rectangles with dots

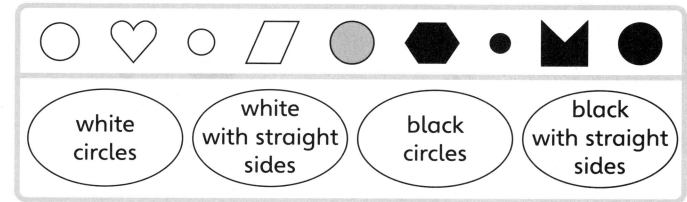

white circles   white with straight sides   black circles   black with straight sides

Sorting Rules

☐ Find one word that describes the data.

_____shirts_____

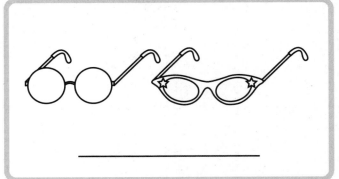

_____

_____

_____

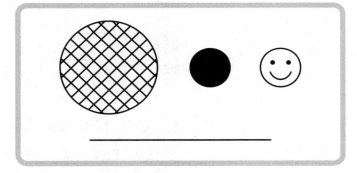

_____

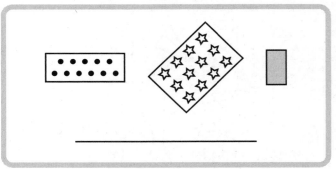

_____

☐ Find two words that describe the data.

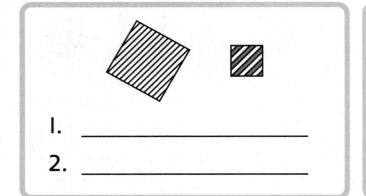

1. _____

2. _____

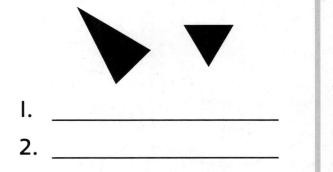

1. _____

2. _____

Probability and Data Management 2-3

☐ How were these sorted? Write two properties.

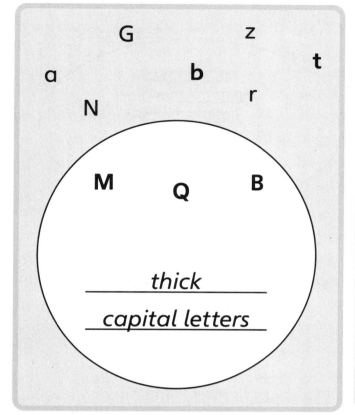

thick

capital letters

_____

_____

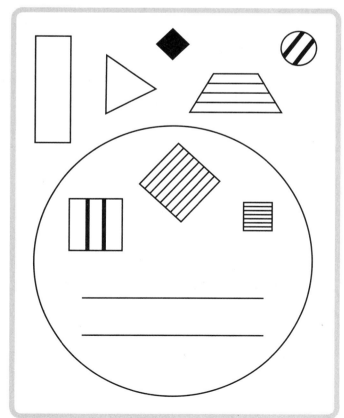

_____

_____

_____

_____

Probability and Data Management 2-3

Sorting Rules—Many Groups

☐ How were these sorted?

new pencils
long

used pencils
short

Bonus

hop   pop   top

November   September

☐ How were these sorted?

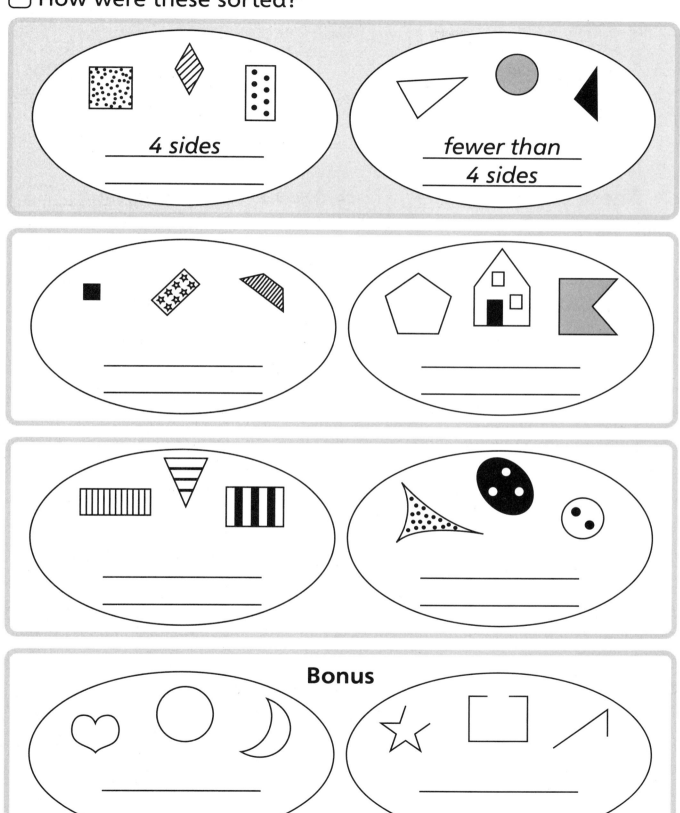

4 sides

_____

fewer than
4 sides

Bonus

☐ Compare the groups.

____red____   ____yellow____   ____green____

These are all __foods__. They are sorted by __colour__.

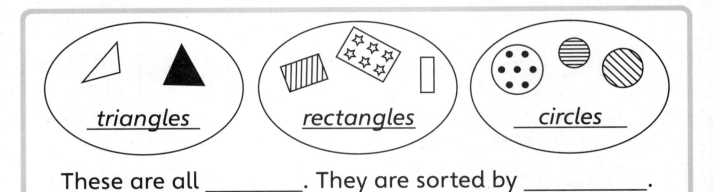

__triangles__   __rectangles__   __circles__

These are all _____. They are sorted by _____.

_____   _____   _____

These are all _____. They are sorted by _____.

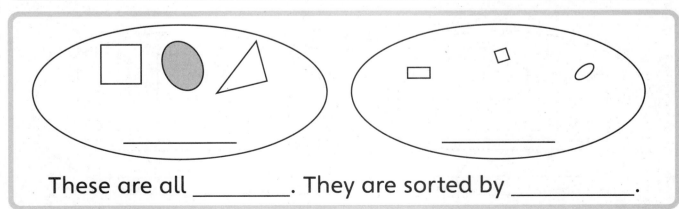

_____   _____

These are all _____. They are sorted by _____.

Probability and Data Management 2-4

geometric properties	not geometric properties
has 4 vertices	large dotted
has 6 sides	fluffy thick
has curved sides	pink
is a triangle	has a pattern
all sides are equal	its name starts with "s"

☐ Circle the geometric properties.

curly	small	made of wood
has 5 sides	pretty	has 3 vertices
is a rectangle	blue	has 7 dots

☐ Write **geometric** or **not geometric**.

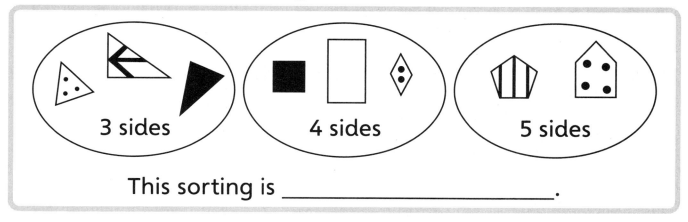

This sorting is _____.

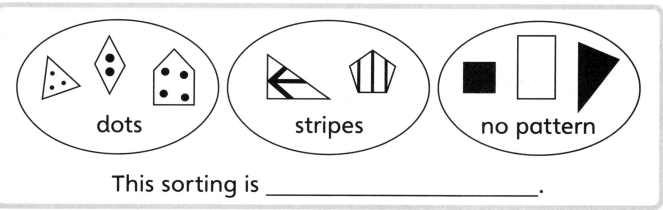

This sorting is _____.

Sort and Graph

☐ Sort the data.
☐ Write the sorted data in the correct rows.

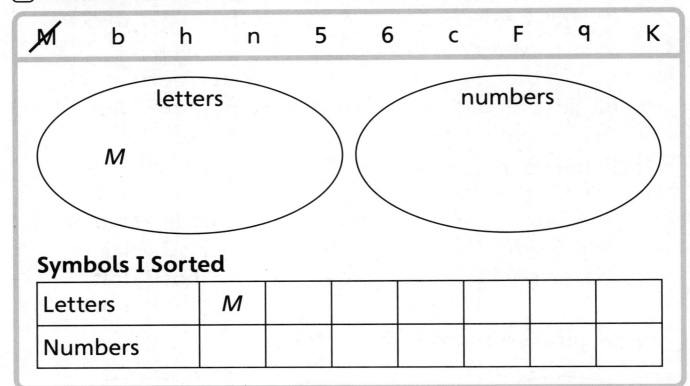

| M | b | h | n | 5 | 6 | c | F | q | K |

letters

M

numbers

Symbols I Sorted

Letters	M						
Numbers							

| am | bat | sit | on | two | or | day |

3 letters

2 letters

Words in My List

3 letters				
2 letters				

Pictographs

Lunch Time

| At home | ☺ ☺ ☺ ☺ ☺ ☺ | ___6___ eat at home |
| At school | ☺ ☺ ☺ ☺ | ___4___ eat at school |

More students eat lunch ___*at home*___ .

Mitts or Gloves

| Mitts | 🧤 🧤 🧤 🧤 🧤 | _____ wear mitts |
| Gloves | ✋ ✋ ✋ | _____ wear gloves |

More students wear _____ .

Sally's Clothes

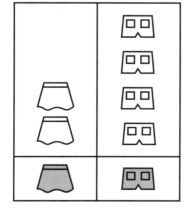

Sally has ____ skirts.

Sally has ____ shorts.

Sally has fewer _____

than _____ .

Marko's Flowers

| Tulips | Roses | Daisies |

____ tulips

____ roses

____ daisies

Marko has the same number of _____ and _____ .

How many more?

Students' Ages

| 7-year-olds | 유 | 유 | 유 | 유 | | | | 4 | _7-year-olds_ |
| 8-year-olds | 유 | 유 | 유 | 유 | 유 | 유 | 유 | 7 | _8-year-olds_ |

__7__ − __4__ = __3__ more

There are __3__ more 8-year-olds than 7-year-olds.

Shoes

| Running shoes | 유 | 유 | 유 | 유 | 유 | 유 | 유 | 유 | | _____ |
| Boots | 유 | 유 | 유 | 유 | | | | | | _____ |

_____ − _____ = _____ fewer

_____ fewer people wear boots than running shoes.

Birds We Saw

| Pigeons | 🐦 | 🐦 | 🐦 | | | | | _____ |
| Robins | 🐦 | 🐦 | 🐦 | 🐦 | 🐦 | | | _____ |

_____ − _____ = _____ fewer

We saw _____ fewer pigeons than robins.

Pet Owners

| Have a pet | 유 | 유 | 유 | 유 | 유 | 유 | 유 | 유 | | _____ |
| Have no pet | 유 | 유 | 유 | 유 | 유 | 유 | 유 | | | _____ |

_____ − _____ = _____ more

_____ more children have a pet than do not.

Probability and Data Management 2-6

○ Use the pictograph to fill in the blanks.

Shoes We Wore Today

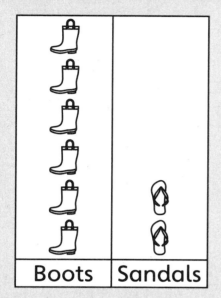

| Boots | Sandals |

| 6 | _people in boots_ |

| 2 | _people in sandals_ |

| 6 | + | 2 | = | 8 | in total

__8__ people altogether

Goals Scored

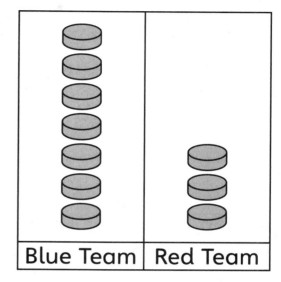

| Blue Team | Red Team |

☐ _____

☐ _____

☐ + ☐ = ☐ in total

____ goals scored in total

Favourite After-School Club

Art	☺ ☺ ☺ ☺ ☺ ☺	☐ _____
Sports	☺ ☺ ☺ ☺ ☺ ☺ ☺ ☺ ☺	☐ _____
Music	☺ ☺ ☺	☐ _____

___ + ___ + ___ = _____ altogether

_____ students go to after-school clubs.

Drawing Pictographs

☐ Use the graphs to answer the questions.

Lunch in Ms. Lee's Class

At school	S	S	S	S	S	S	S						
At home	H	H	H	H	H	H	H	H	H	H	H	H	H

More students in Ms. Lee's class eat lunch

_____ than _____.

Lunch in Mr. King's Class

At school	S	S		S	S		S	S		S	S		
At home	H	H	H	H	H	H		H	H	H			

Mr. King's students think **more** of them eat at school

than at home. Is that correct? _____

Fix the graph so that it is easier to read.

At school													
At home													

☐ Use data from the graphs above.

Lunch at School

Ms. Lee's class													
Mr. King's class													

Which teacher has more students eating at school? _____

How many more? _____

Probability and Data Management 2-7

☐ Draw ☺ to show the data.
☐ Answer the questions.

Favourite Ball Games

Soccer	☺	☺	☺	☺	☺
Basketball					
Baseball					

5 like soccer the most.

3 like basketball the most.

4 like baseball the most.

How many more students like soccer the most than like baseball the most? _____

Shoes We Wear

Running shoes					
Boots					

5 wear running shoes.

2 wear boots.

4 wear sandals.

How many fewer students wear boots than sandals? _____

Kate asked friends where they will be during March break.

Title: _____

Camp	
Do not know	

5 will go to camp.

3 will stay at home.

2 will go to a cottage.

4 do not know.

How many friends did Kate ask? _____

☐ Write one thing you learned from Kate's graph.

Counting to 100

How many crayons?

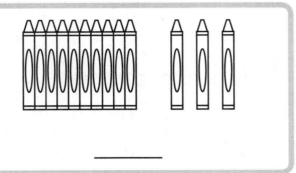

_____

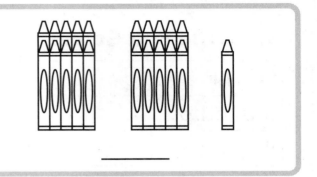

_____

_____

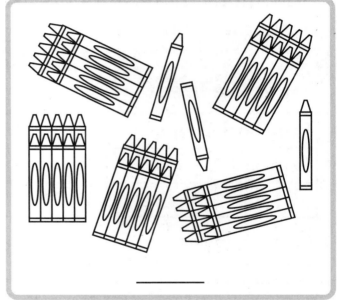

_____

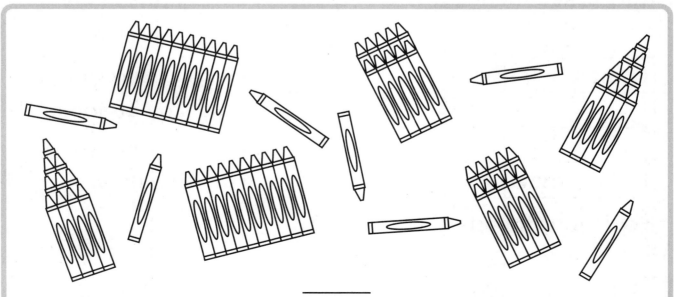

_____

⬜ Count the groups of tens and ones.
⬜ Write the number.

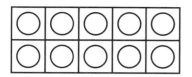 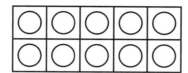 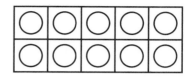

_____

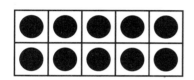 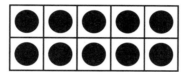 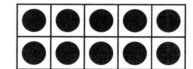

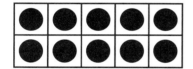 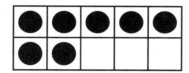

_____

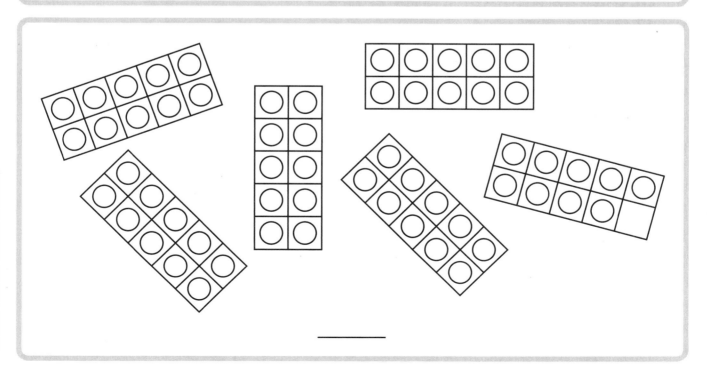

_____

Hundreds Charts

Sam is looking for numbers in the hundreds chart.

◯ Colour where he should start.

Find 58 using grey.	Find 90 using green.
Find 87 using red.	Find 65 using yellow.
Find 62 using blue.	Find 71 using orange.

1	2	3	4	5	6	7	8	9	10

◯ Shade the number in the chart.
◯ Write what comes next and what comes before.

74 75 76	____ 79 ____	____ 90 ____
____ 81 ____	____ 82 ____	____ 96 ____

71	72	73	74	75	76	77	78	79	80
81	82	83	84	85	86	87	88	89	90
91	92	93	94	95	96	97	98	99	100

More Tens and Ones Blocks

◯ Fill in the blanks.

1	2	3	4	5	6	7	8	9	10
11	12	13	14	15	16	17	18	19	20
21	22	23	24	25	26	27	28	29	30
31	32	33	34	35	36	37	38	39	40

32 = _____ tens
     + _____ ones

1	2	3	4	5	6	7	8	9	10
11	12	13	14	15	16	17	18	19	20
21	22	23	24	25	26	27	28	29	30
31	32	33	34	35	36	37	38	39	40

34 = _____ tens
     + _____ ones

◯ Place tens and ones blocks on the chart to show the number.
◯ Fill in the blanks.

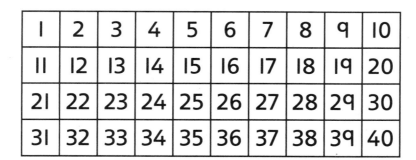

1	2	3	4	5	6	7	8	9	10
11	12	13	14	15	16	17	18	19	20
21	22	23	24	25	26	27	28	29	30
31	32	33	34	35	36	37	38	39	40

28 is _____ tens blocks and _____ ones blocks.

27 is _____ tens blocks and _____ ones blocks.

23 is _____ tens blocks and _____ ones blocks.

35 is _____ tens blocks and _____ ones blocks.

30 is _____ tens blocks and _____ ones blocks.

▤ Lela says 32 and 23 mean the same thing.
   Is she correct? Explain.

◯ Fill in the table.
◯ Write the number.

tens	ones
3	4

Number: __34__

tens	ones

Number: _____

tens	ones

Number: _____

tens	ones

Number: _____

▤ Use blocks to show each number.   50   43   37   19   32

How many ones altogether?

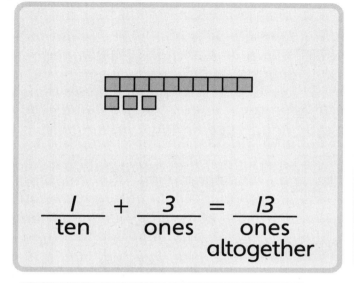

$$\underline{\quad 1 \quad} + \underline{\quad 3 \quad} = \underline{\quad 13 \quad}$$
ten   ones   ones altogether

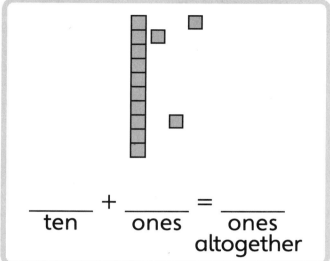

$$\underline{\qquad} + \underline{\qquad} = \underline{\qquad}$$
ten   ones   ones altogether

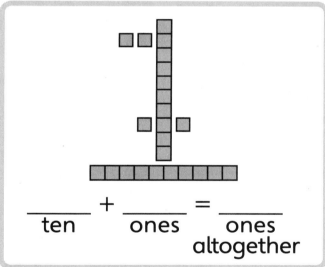

$$\underline{\qquad} + \underline{\qquad} = \underline{\qquad}$$
ten   ones   ones altogether

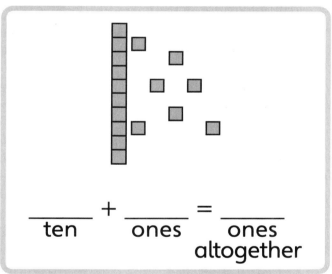

$$\underline{\qquad} + \underline{\qquad} = \underline{\qquad}$$
ten   ones   ones altogether

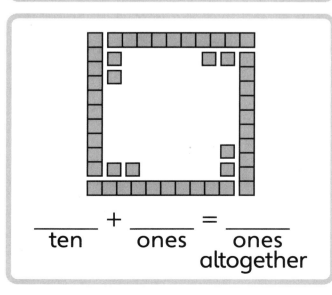

$$\underline{\qquad} + \underline{\qquad} = \underline{\qquad}$$
ten   ones   ones altogether

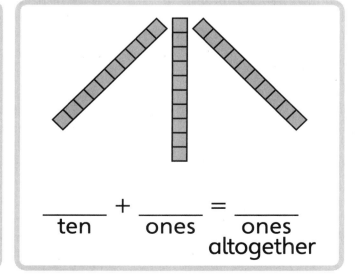

$$\underline{\qquad} + \underline{\qquad} = \underline{\qquad}$$
ten   ones   ones altogether

Ordering Numbers to 100

☐ Circle the largest number.

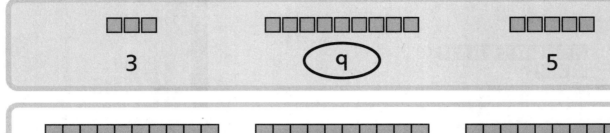

3   (9)   5

13   19   15

23   29   25

33 39 35	43 49 45
73 75 79	99 93 95

☐ Write the numbers in order from largest to smallest.

4 7 6 _7_ ____ ____	34 37 36 ____ ____ ____
49 43 44 ____ ____ ____	82 80 85 ____ ____ ____

☐ Circle two numbers that are out of order.   51   55   58   57   59

     Number Sense 2-21

☐ Circle the largest number.

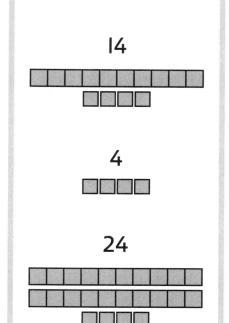

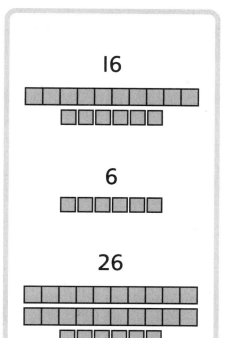

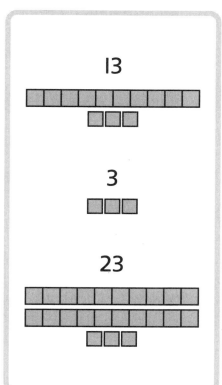

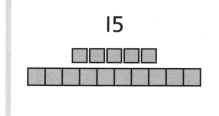

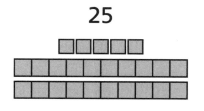

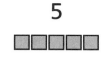

| 34 | 74 | 54 |

| 29 | 19 | 89 |

☐ Write the numbers in order from largest to smallest.

| 53 | 63 | 43 |

_63_ _____ _____

| 27 | 7 | 37 |

_____ _____ _____

☐ Circle two numbers that are out of order. 24 44 84 74 94

◯ Circle the larger number.

10	9

20	19

30 29	49 50	80 79

39 40	60 59	90 89

15	20

30	26

47 50	60 53	80 90

50 40	30 26	20 70

☐ Write the numbers in order.

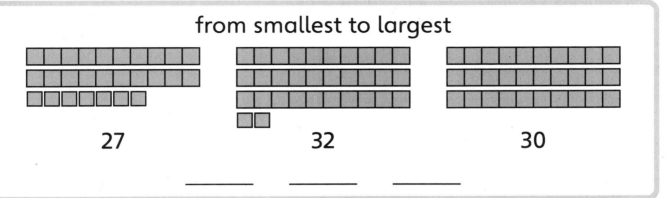

from smallest to largest

27   32   30

_____   _____   _____

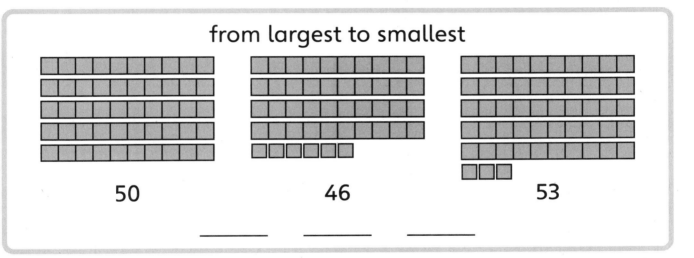

from largest to smallest

50   46   53

_____   _____   _____

☐ Write the numbers from smallest to largest.

57	61	50
_____	_____	_____

23	18	20
_____	_____	_____

51	94	8	48	19	49	20
_____	_____	_____	_____	_____	_____	_____

Aki tried to write the numbers from smallest to largest.

☐ Circle Aki's mistakes.

23	25	34	30	41

54	73	68	75	80

Circle the numbers on the number line.

Write the numbers from smallest to largest.

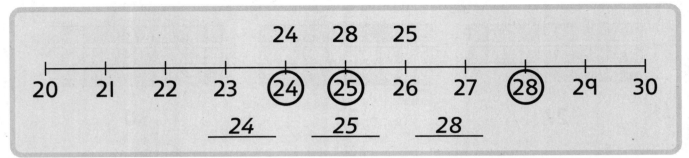

24   28   25

20 21 22 23 (24) (25) 26 27 (28) 29 30

                24   25   28

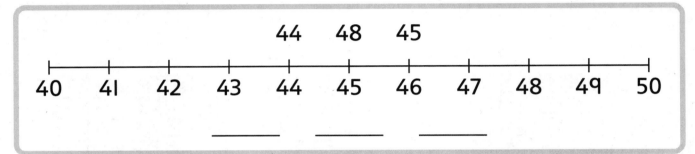

44   48   45

40 41 42 43 44 45 46 47 48 49 50

_____   _____   _____

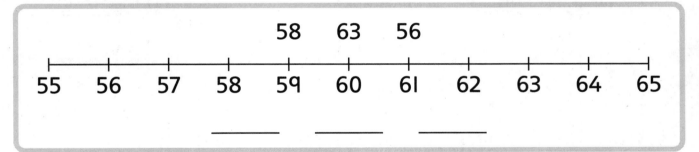

58   63   56

55 56 57 58 59 60 61 62 63 64 65

_____   _____   _____

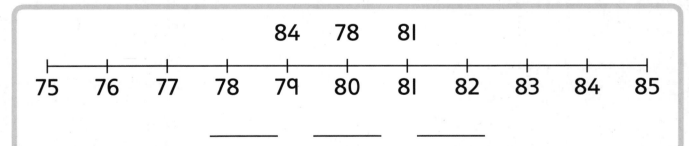

84   78   81

75 76 77 78 79 80 81 82 83 84 85

_____   _____   _____

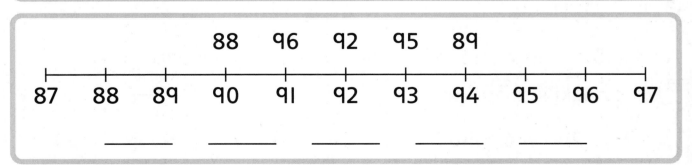

88   96   92   95   89

87 88 89 90 91 92 93 94 95 96 97

_____   _____   _____

⬜ Write the shaded numbers in order.
Start with the smallest number.

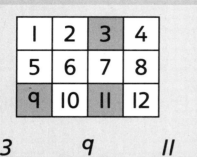

1	2	**3**	4
5	6	7	8
9	10	**11**	12

__3__   __9__   __11__

1	**2**	3	4
5	6	**7**	8
9	10	11	12

_____ _____ _____

31	32	33	**34**	35
36	37	38	39	40
41	42	**43**	44	45

_____ _____ _____

53	54	**55**	56	57
58	59	60	61	**62**
63	**64**	65	66	67

_____ _____ _____

65	**66**	67	68	69	70	71	**72**	73	74
75	76	**77**	78	79	**80**	81	82	83	**84**
85	86	87	88	89	**90**	91	92	93	94

_____ _____ _____ _____ _____ _____ _____

1	2	**3**	4	5	6	7	8	9	**10**
11	12	13	14	15	**16**	17	18	19	20
21	22	23	24	**25**	26	27	28	**29**	**30**

_____ _____ _____ _____ _____ _____ _____

⬜ Use a metre stick to check your answers.

The > sign means **greater than**.

☐ Fill in the number sentence.

1. 7 is greater than 3.

__7__ > __3__

2. 19 is greater than 8.

_____ > _____

3. 72 is greater than 41.

_____ > _____

4. 37 is greater than 4.

_____ > _____

5. 62 is greater than 26.

_____ > _____

6. 55 is greater than 47.

_____ > _____

☐ Circle **yes** or **no**.

7. 87 > 19

(yes)   no

8. 17 > 21

yes   no

9. 36 > 31

yes   no

10. 57 > 50

yes   no

11. 42 > 91

yes   no

12. 51 > 16

yes   no

13. 61 > 78

yes   no

14. 40 > 60

yes   no

15. 92 > 8

yes   no

16. 23 > 41

yes   no

17. 35 > 16

yes   no

18. 53 > 68

yes   no

☐ Circle the greater number.
☐ Write the numbers in the correct places.

19.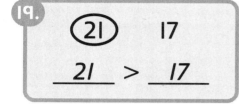
(21)　　17

__21__ > __17__

20.
32　　(57)

__57__ > __32__

21.
8　　　90

_____ > _____

22.
15　　80

_____ > _____

23.
33　　2

_____ > _____

24.
42　　81

_____ > _____

25.
61　　30

_____ > _____

26.
85　　96

_____ > _____

27.
77　　52

_____ > _____

☐ Circle the greater amount.
☐ Write the numbers in the correct places.

28.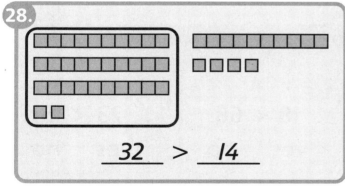

__32__ > __14__

29.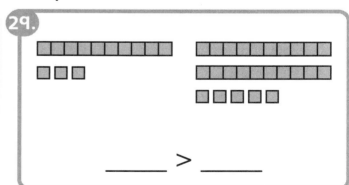

_____ > _____

30.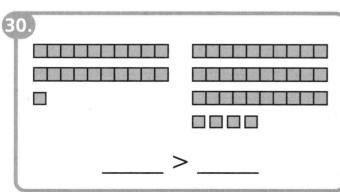

_____ > _____

31.

_____ > _____

The < sign means **less than**.

☐ Fill in the number sentence.

1.

12 is less than 32.

_12_ **<** _32_

2.

19 is less than 97.

____ < ____

3.

18 is less than 58.

____ < ____

4.

82 is less than 90.

____ < ____

5.

67 is less than 74.

____ < ____

6.

59 is less than 65.

____ < ____

☐ Circle **yes** or **no**.

7. 82 < 21
yes   (no)

8. 91 < 97
yes   no

9. 18 < 68
yes   no

10. 23 < 16
yes   no

11. 40 < 49
yes   no

12. 91 < 95
yes   no

13. 82 < 17
yes   no

14. 78 < 12
yes   no

15. 6 < 11
yes   no

16. 2 < 60
yes   no

17. 35 < 9
yes   no

18. 82 < 43
yes   no

☐ Circle the number that is less.

☐ Write the numbers in the correct places.

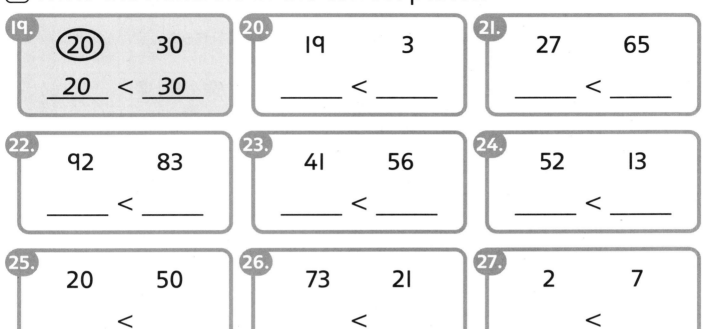

19. (20) 30

___20___ < ___30___

20. 19   3

_____ < _____

21. 27   65

_____ < _____

22. 92   83

_____ < _____

23. 41   56

_____ < _____

24. 52   13

_____ < _____

25. 20   50

_____ < _____

26. 73   21

_____ < _____

27. 2   7

_____ < _____

☐ Circle the smaller amount.

☐ Write the numbers in the correct places.

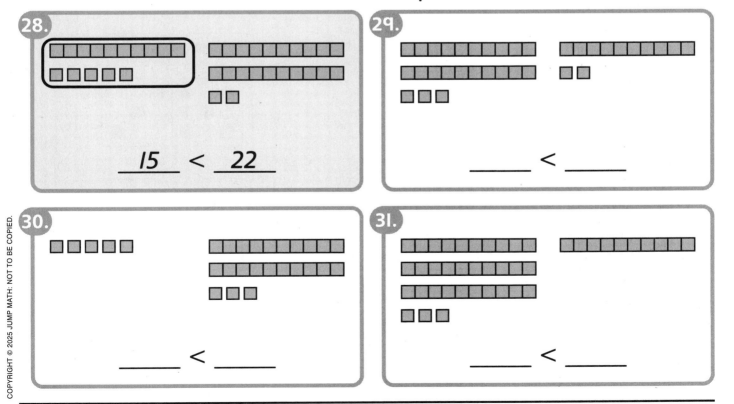

28.

___15___ < ___22___

29.

_____ < _____

30.

_____ < _____

31.

_____ < _____

Adding, Subtracting, and Order

The dominoes got turned around.

☐ Write one addition sentence for both pictures.

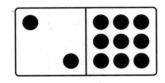

__2__ + __5__ = __7__ = __5__ + __2__

__ + __ = __ = __ + __

__ + __ = __ = __ + __

__ + __ = __ = __ + __

__ + __ = __ = __ + __

 Randi says 34 + 17 = 17 + 34. Explain why she is correct.

How many buttons altogether?

☐ Find the total in 6 different ways.

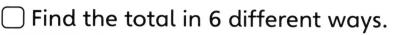

total

__10__ = __2__ + __5__ + __3__

total

____ = ____ + ____ + ____

total

____ = ____ + ____ + ____

total

____ = ____ + ____ + ____

total

____ = ____ + ____ + ____

total

____ = ____ + ____ + ____

What does the subtraction mean?

☐ Use the picture to subtract.

5 − 2 means _____*take 2 away from 5*_____

◯ ◯ ◯ ⊗ ⊗   5 − 2 = __3__

7 − 4 means _____

◯ ◯ ◯ ◯ ◯ ◯ ◯   7 − 4 = ____

8 − 3 means _____

◯ ◯ ◯ ◯ ◯ ◯ ◯ ◯   8 − 3 = ____

☐ Can you take 5 away from 3? ◯ ◯ ◯ yes / no
Does 3 − 5 make sense? yes / no

☐ Solve the problem that makes sense.

3 − 6 = ___ or 6 − 3 = ___   9 − 2 = ___ or 2 − 9 = ___

4 − 8 = ___ or 8 − 4 = ___   10 − 5 = ___ or 5 − 10 = ___

⌇☐ Which problem makes sense, 3 − 7 or 7 − 3? Explain.

OA2-12 Distance from 0 on a Number Line

☐ Circle the correct number line.

1.

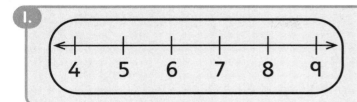 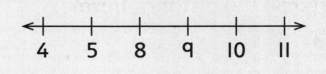

2.

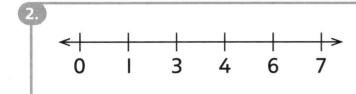 

3.

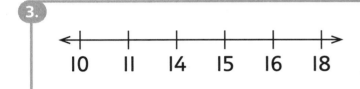 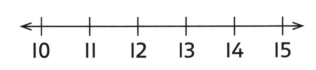

The frog starts at 0.

☐ Number each jump.

☐ Circle the distance from 0.

4.

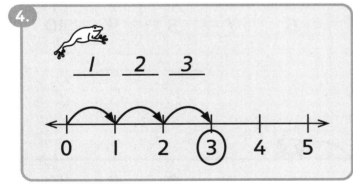

5.

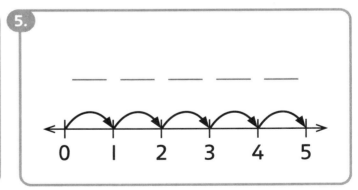

6.

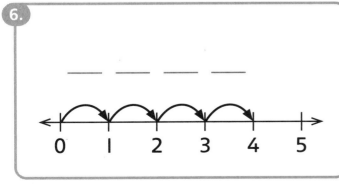

7.

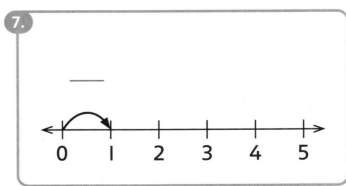

How many jumps away from 0 is the frog?

☐ Number each jump.
☐ Circle the distance from 0.

8.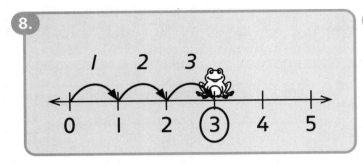

9.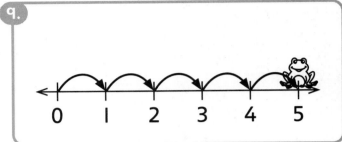

10.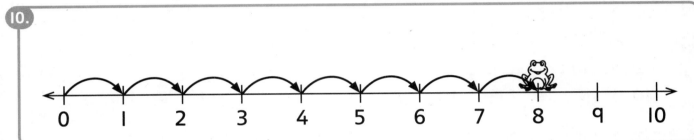

11.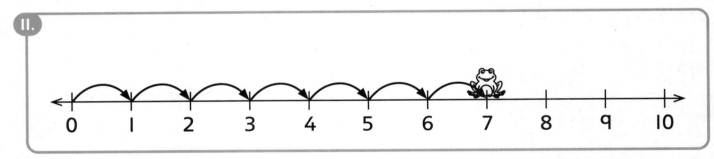

12.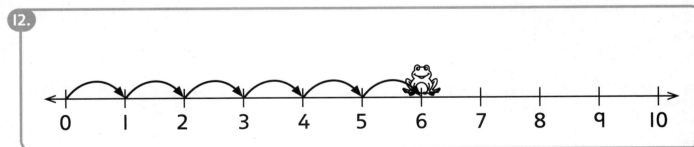

13.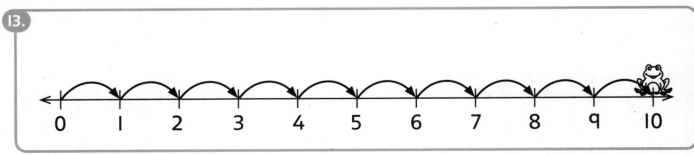

Operations and Algebraic Thinking 2-12

Adding with a Number Line

The frog takes 2 leaps. Where does it end up?

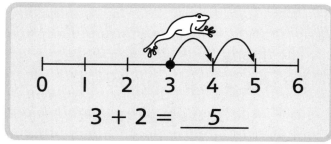

$3 + 2 = \underline{\quad 5 \quad}$

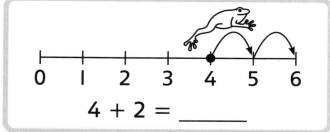

$4 + 2 = \underline{\qquad}$

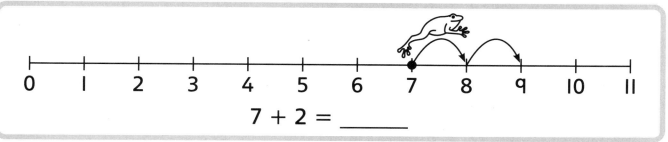

$7 + 2 = \underline{\qquad}$

☐ Trace 3 leaps.
☐ Add 3.

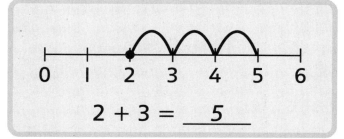

$2 + 3 = \underline{\quad 5 \quad}$

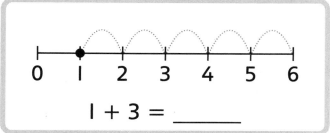

$1 + 3 = \underline{\qquad}$

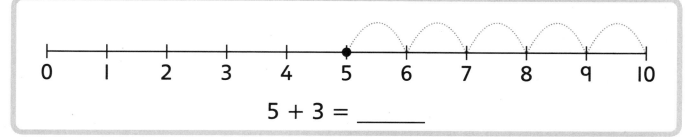

$5 + 3 = \underline{\qquad}$

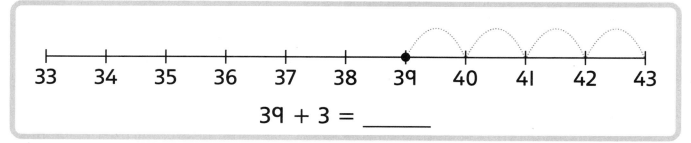

$39 + 3 = \underline{\qquad}$

The frog starts at the first number.

◯ Draw a dot where the frog starts.

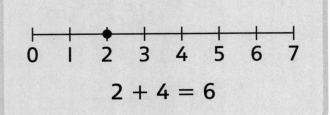

2 + 4 = 6

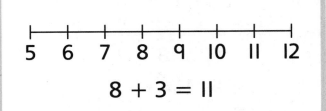

8 + 3 = 11

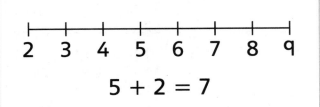

5 + 2 = 7

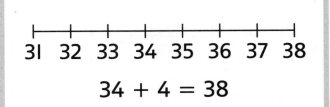

34 + 4 = 38

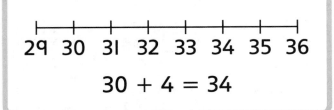

30 + 4 = 34

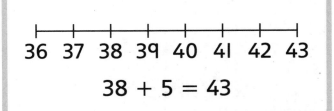

38 + 5 = 43

The frog jumps the second number of leaps.

◯ Draw the frog's leaps.

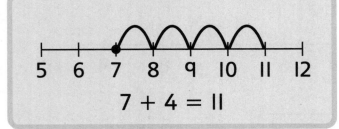

7 + 4 = 11

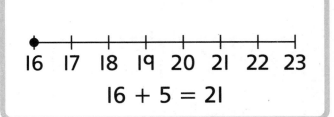

16 + 5 = 21

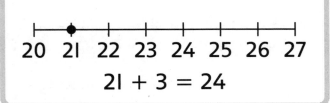

21 + 3 = 24

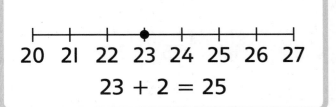

23 + 2 = 25

☐ Use the number line to add.

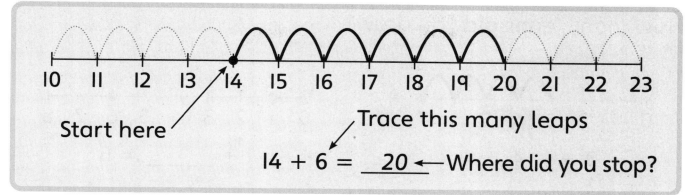

Start here

Trace this many leaps

$14 + 6 =$ ___20___ ←Where did you stop?

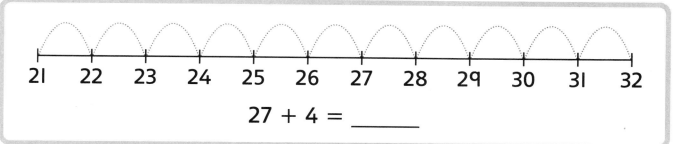

$27 + 4 =$ _____

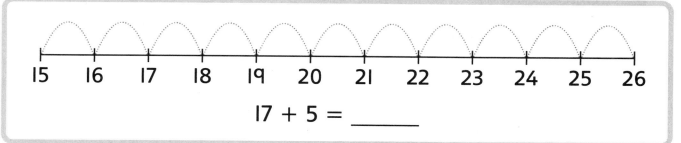

$17 + 5 =$ _____

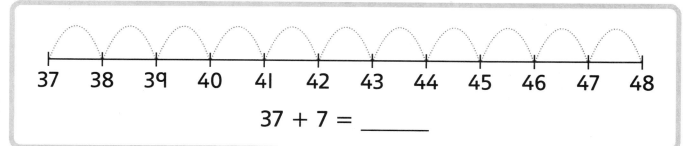

$37 + 7 =$ _____

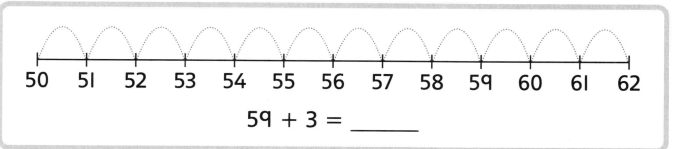

$59 + 3 =$ _____

⬜ Draw the leaps from the first dot to the second dot.

How many leaps did you draw?

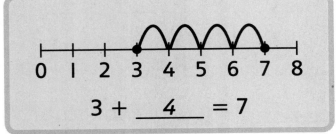

3 + __4__ = 7

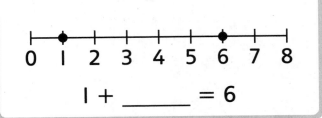

1 + _____ = 6

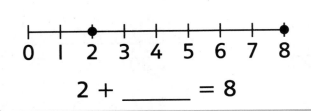

2 + _____ = 8

22 + _____ = 25

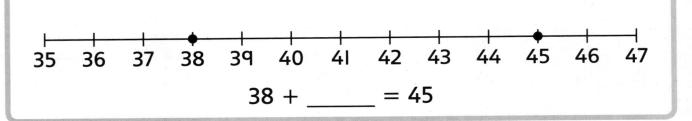

38 + _____ = 45

⬜ Use the number line to find the missing number.

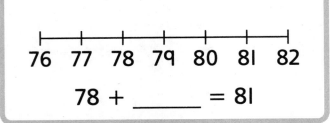

78 + _____ = 81

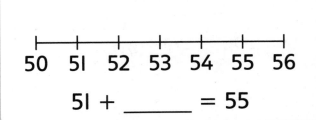

51 + _____ = 55

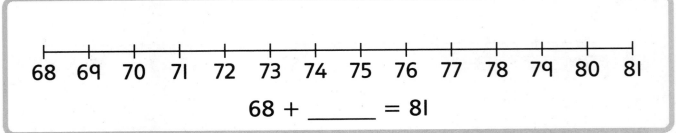

68 + _____ = 81

Adding by Counting On

☐ Colour the next circle.
☐ Add 1.

1	2	3	4	5	6	7	8	9	10	11	12
●	●	●	●	●	●	●	●	●	○	○	○

$8 + 1 = \underline{\quad 9 \quad}$

1	2	3	4	5	6	7	8	9	10	11	12
●	●	●	●	●	●	●	●	●	●	○	○

$10 + 1 = \underline{\qquad}$

1	2	3	4	5	6	7	8	9	10	11	12
●	●	●	●	●	○	○	○	○	○	○	○

$5 + 1 = \underline{\qquad}$

☐ Find the next number.
☐ Add 1.

1 2 3 **4** 5 6 7

$4 + 1 = \underline{\qquad}$

1 2 3 4 5 **6** 7

$6 + 1 = \underline{\qquad}$

$9 + 1 = \underline{\qquad}$

$11 + 1 = \underline{\qquad}$

$17 + 1 = \underline{\qquad}$

☐ Find the next 2 numbers.
☐ Add 2.

1   2   3   **4**   5   6   7   8

4 + 2 = ___6___

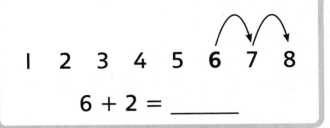

1   2   3   4   5   **6**   7   8

6 + 2 = _____

1   2   **3**   4   5   6   7   8

3 + 2 = _____

1   2   3   4   **5**   6   7   8

5 + 2 = _____

☐ Write the next 2 numbers to add 2.

7   ____   ____   so 7 + 2 = ____

15   ____   ____   so 15 + 2 = ____

89   ____   ____   so 89 + 2 = ____

☐ Write the next 5 numbers to add 5.

2   ____   ____   ____   ____   ____   so 2 + 5 = ____

18   ____   ____   ____   ____   ____   so 18 + 5 = ____

☐ Start at the first number.
☐ Trace the second number of blanks.
☐ Add by counting on.

| 5 | _6_ | _7_ | _8_ | _9_ | _10_ | _11_ | .... | 5 + 6 = _11_ |

| ☐ | ------- ------- ------- ------- ------- ------- ------- | 8 + 2 = ___ |

| ☐ | ------- ------- ------- ------- ------- ------- ------- | 21 + 4 = ___ |

☐ Use your fingers to add by counting on.

| 37 | _38_ | _39_ | _40_ | _41_ | so 37 + 4 = 41 |

45 + 3 = _____   58 + 4 = _____   69 + 2 = _____

38 + 3 = _____   29 + 2 = _____   35 + 4 = _____

84 + 9 = _____   75 + 7 = _____   57 + 7 = _____

☐ Trace the correct number of blanks.
☐ Add by counting on in 2 ways.

$7 + 3 =$ ___10___

7 __8__ __9__ __10__ ....

3 __4__ __5__ __6__ __7__ __8__ __9__ __10__ ....

$2 + 5 =$ _____

2 ....

5 ....

$9 + 3 =$ _____

9 ....

3 ....

$4 + 8 =$ _____

4 ....

8 ....

☐ What is easier, counting on from the **bigger** number or from the **smaller** number? Explain.

_____

_____

_____

Subtracting with a Number Line

The frog takes 2 leaps back. Where does it end up?

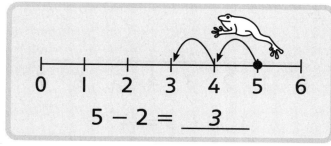

$5 - 2 = \underline{\quad 3 \quad}$

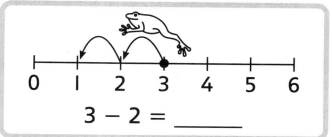

$3 - 2 = \underline{\qquad}$

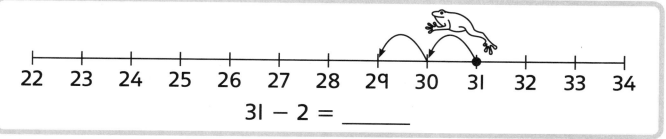

$31 - 2 = \underline{\qquad}$

☐ Trace 3 leaps back.
☐ Subtract 3.

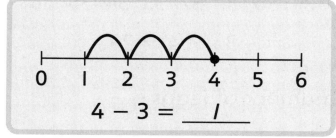

$4 - 3 = \underline{\quad 1 \quad}$

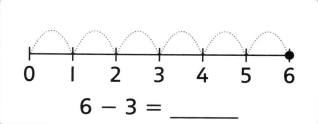

$6 - 3 = \underline{\qquad}$

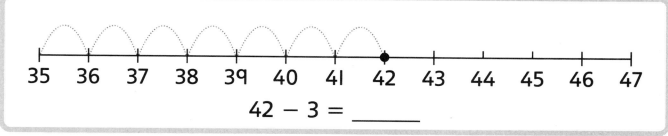

$42 - 3 = \underline{\qquad}$

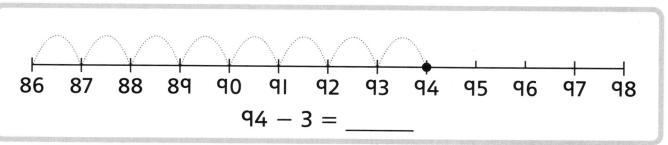

$94 - 3 = \underline{\qquad}$

The frog starts at the first number.

◯ Draw a dot where the frog starts.

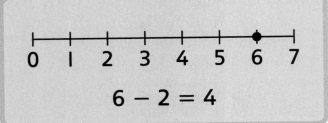

6 − 2 = 4

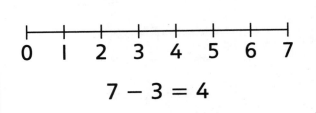

7 − 3 = 4

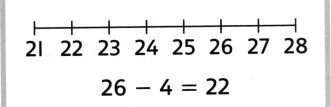

26 − 4 = 22

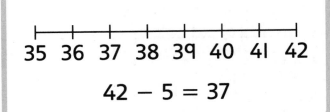

42 − 5 = 37

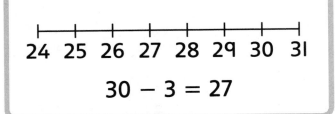

30 − 3 = 27

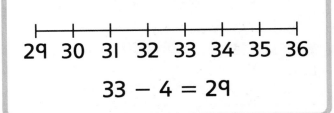

33 − 4 = 29

The frog jumps back the second number of leaps.

◯ Draw the frog's leaps.

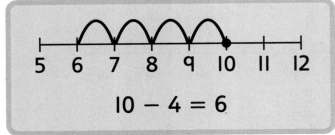

10 − 4 = 6

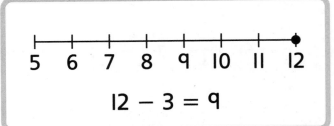

12 − 3 = 9

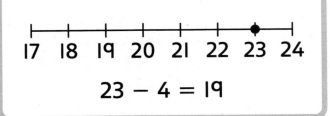

23 − 4 = 19

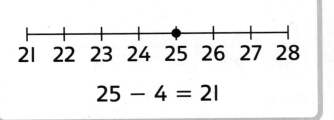

25 − 4 = 21

☐ Use the number line to subtract.

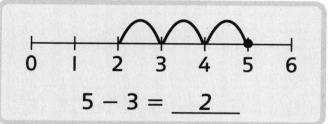

$5 - 3 = \underline{\quad 2 \quad}$

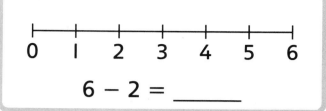

$6 - 2 = \underline{\qquad}$

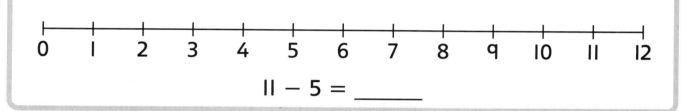

$11 - 5 = \underline{\qquad}$

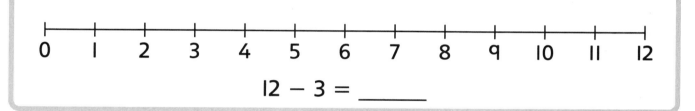

$12 - 3 = \underline{\qquad}$

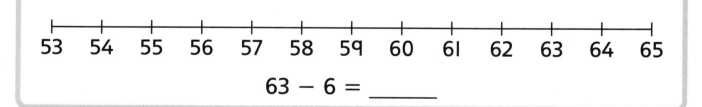

$63 - 6 = \underline{\qquad}$

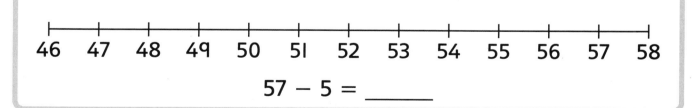

$57 - 5 = \underline{\qquad}$

Make your own.

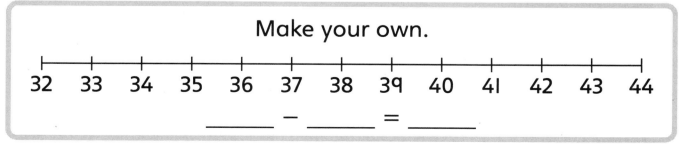

$\underline{\qquad} - \underline{\qquad} = \underline{\qquad}$

☐ Draw the leaps from the second dot to the first dot.
☐ How many leaps did you draw? Fill in the blank.

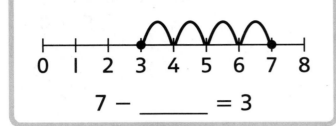

7 − _____ = 3

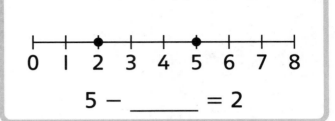

5 − _____ = 2

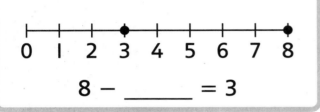

8 − _____ = 3

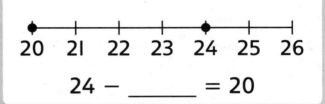

24 − _____ = 20

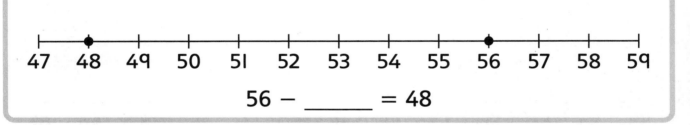

56 − _____ = 48

☐ Use the number line to find the missing number.

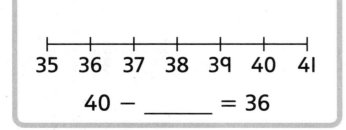

40 − _____ = 36

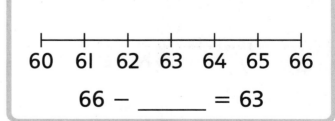

66 − _____ = 63

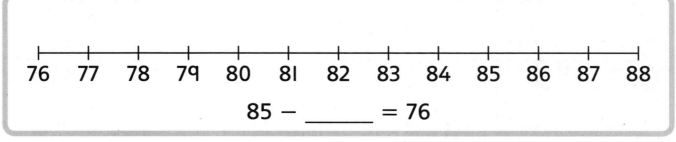

85 − _____ = 76

Use the number line to add or subtract.

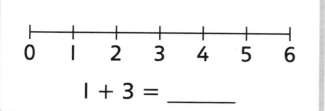

1 + 3 = _____

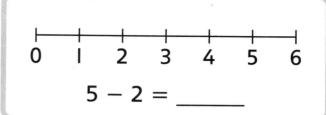

5 − 2 = _____

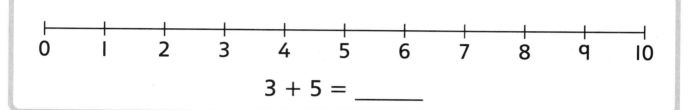

3 + 5 = _____

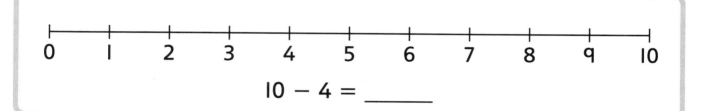

10 − 4 = _____

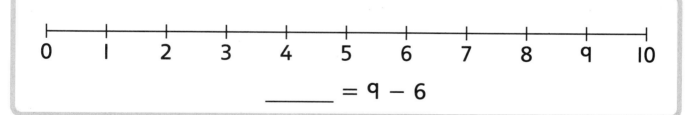

_____ = 9 − 6

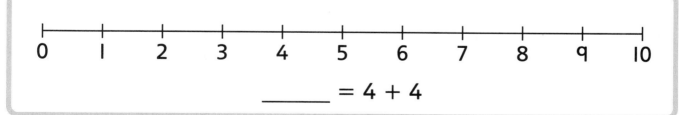

_____ = 4 + 4

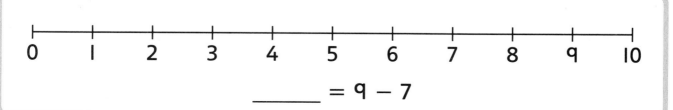

_____ = 9 − 7

Subtracting by Counting Backwards

◯ Subtract by counting back.

8   _7_   _6_   _5_   _4_   _3_ $8 - 5 =$ _3_

6   ___   ___   ___   ___ $6 - 4 =$ _____

28   ___   ___   ___ $28 - 3 =$ _____

132   ___   ___   ___   ___   ___ $132 - 5 =$ _____

◯ Trace the blanks, then subtract.

21   ------   ------   ------   ------   ------ $21 - 2 =$ _____

30   ------   ------   ------   ------   ------ $30 - 5 =$ _____

543   ------   ------   ------   ------   ------ $543 - 4 =$ _____

◯ Keep track on your fingers to subtract.

$28 - 4 =$ _____ $32 - 3 =$ _____ $741 - 2 =$ _____

Subtracting by Counting On

☐ Subtract by counting forwards.

What is 31 − 27?

27   28   29   30   31

27 + __4__ = 31   so   31 − 27 = __4__

---

6 + _____ = 8

so 8 − 6 = _____

---

36 + _____ = 38

so 38 − 36 = _____

---

14 + _____ = 19

so 19 − 14 = _____

---

44 + _____ = 49

so 49 − 44 = _____

---

24 − 18 = _____

52 − 49 = _____

89 − 86 = _____

92 − 88 = _____

93 − 89 = _____

94 − 90 = _____

☐ Make up 3 subtraction questions. Solve them by counting forwards.

◯ Subtract by counting forwards or backwards.

47 − 4 = _____	39 − 36 = _____	42 − 38 = _____
31 − 6 = _____	32 − 25 = _____	33 − 29 = _____
33 − 4 = _____	45 − 7 = _____	41 − 39 = _____
21 − 15 = _____	21 − 3 = _____	46 − 8 = _____
42 − 36 = _____	42 − 5 = _____	37 − 35 = _____
24 − 3 = _____	24 − 19 = _____	37 − 4 = _____
47 − 5 = _____	47 − 2 = _____	47 − 43 = _____

Did you use counting forwards or backwards for the last question? Why?

Make up 3 subtraction questions. Solve them by counting backwards.

Matching Shapes

□ ✓ what is true and ✗ what is not true.

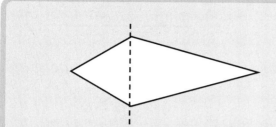

☑ same kind of shape
☒ same size
☒ match exactly

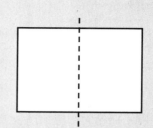

☑ same kind of shape
☑ same size
☑ match exactly

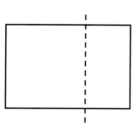

□ same kind of shape
□ same size
□ match exactly

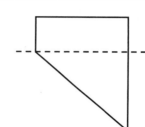

□ same kind of shape
□ same size
□ match exactly

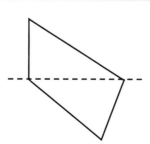

□ same kind of shape
□ same size
□ match exactly

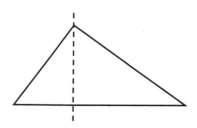

□ same kind of shape
□ same size
□ match exactly

☐ Put an ✗ on the parts that **do not** match exactly.

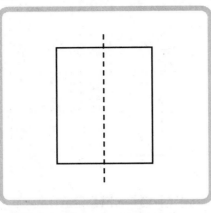 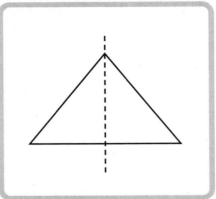 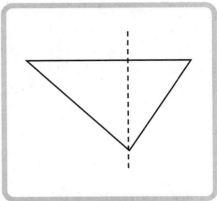

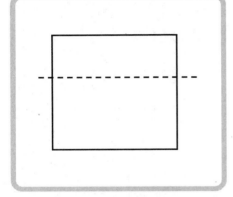 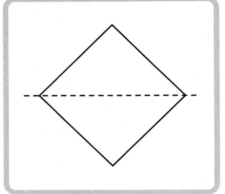 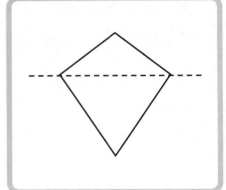

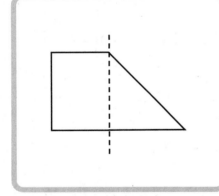 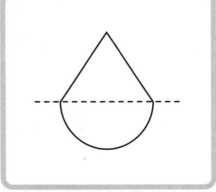 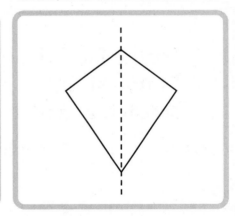

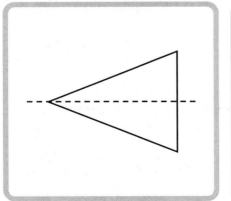 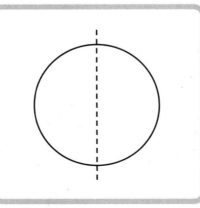

Bonus

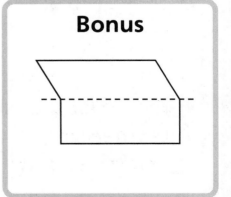

Geometry 2-9

Lines of Symmetry

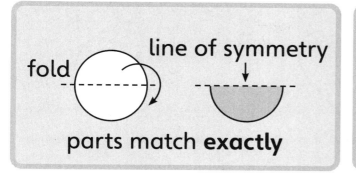
fold — line of symmetry — parts match **exactly**

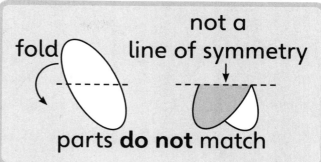
fold — not a line of symmetry — parts **do not** match

Is this a line of symmetry?

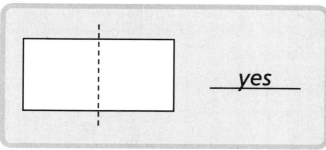
yes

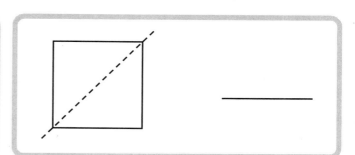
_____

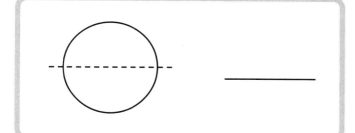
_____

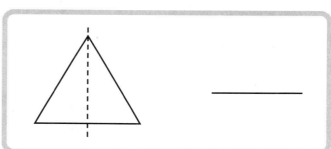
_____

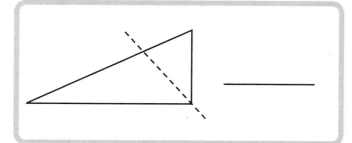
_____

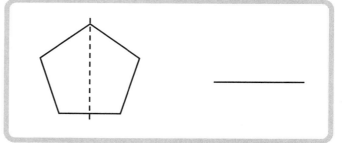
_____

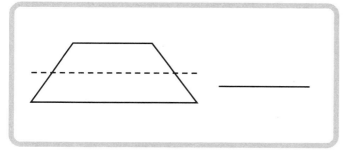
_____

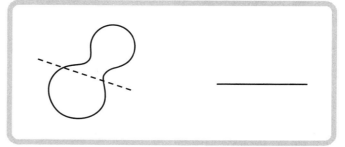
_____

☐ Draw a line of symmetry.

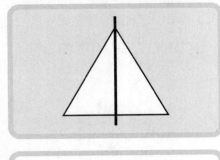

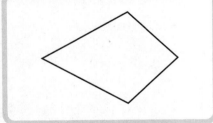
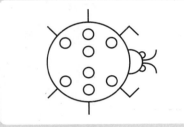
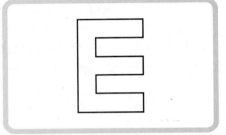

☐ Draw another line of symmetry.

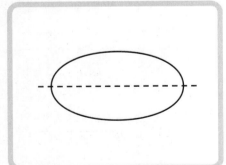
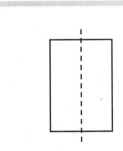
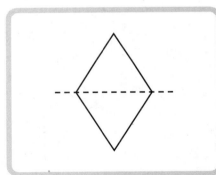

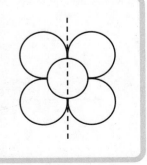
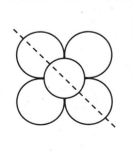

Bonus

Draw 2 more lines of symmetry.

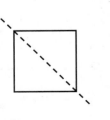

Geometry 2-10

Does this shape have a line of symmetry?
☐ Draw the lines of symmetry you find.

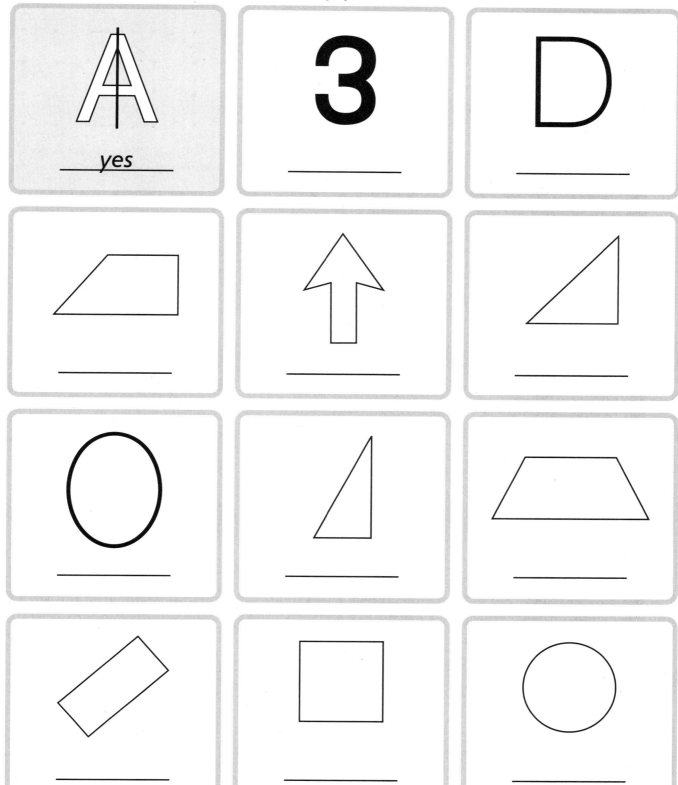

yes

Creating Symmetrical Shapes

☐ Draw the matching part of the symmetrical shape.

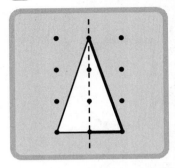 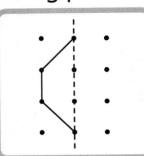 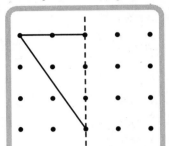 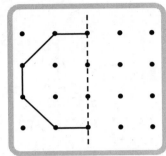

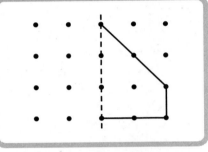 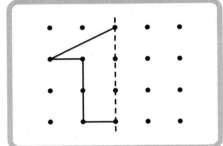 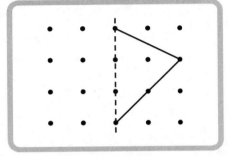

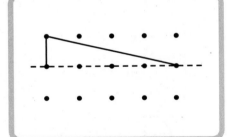 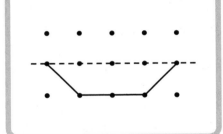 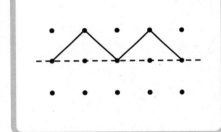

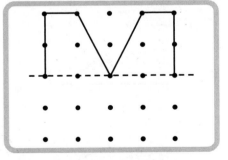 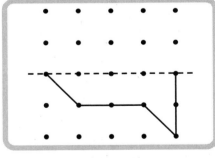 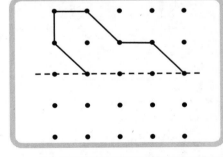

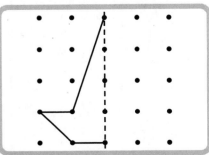 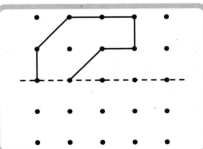 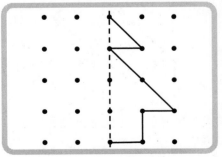

Geometry 2-11

Breaking and Creating Shapes

☐ Draw lines to make the shapes.

2 triangles 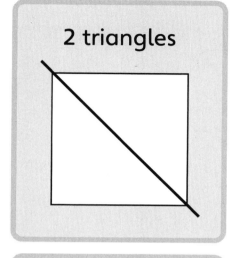	**3 triangles** 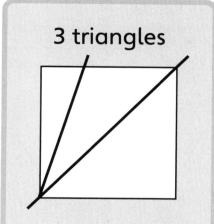	**4 triangles** 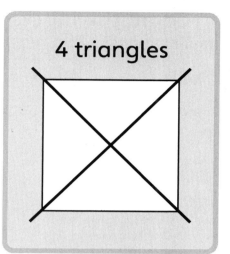
2 rectangles	**4 squares** 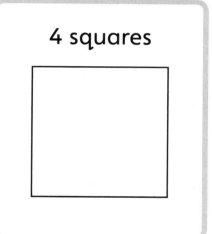	**4 rectangles** 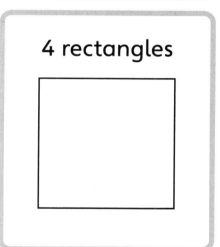
3 rectangles	**4 triangles** 	**8 triangles** 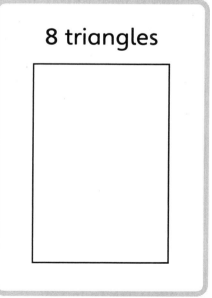

Making Polygons

☐ Cover the bird with pattern blocks. Use different shapes.
☐ Count the blocks you used.

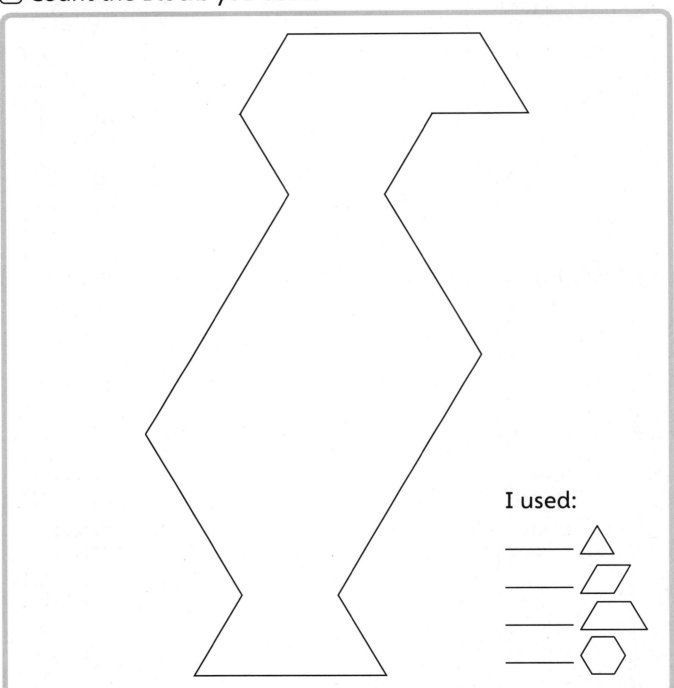

I used:

_____ △

_____ ▱

_____ ⬭

_____ ⬡

☐ Cover the bird with triangles only.
☐ How many triangles? _____ △.

Karen places shapes one on top of the other. She tries to make the shapes match.

If they match exactly, the shapes are **congruent**.

Congruent shapes have the same size and shape.

Congruent shapes   Not congruent shapes

1. Are the shapes congruent? Write "yes" or "no."

a)

_no_

b)

_____

c)

_____

d)

_____

e)

_____

f)

_____

g)

_____

h)

_____

2. Find the 2 congruent shapes. Circle them.

a)

b)

c)

d)

3. Circle the 2 congruent shapes.

a)

b)

c)

d)

Congruent shapes have the same size and shape. They can have different colours, designs, or directions.

4. Draw X on the shape that is not congruent to the other two.

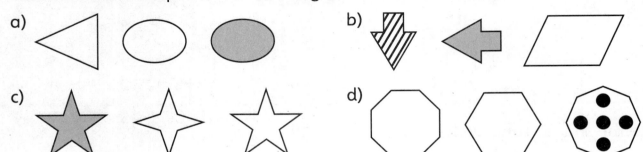

5. Find the dark shape that is congruent to the light shape. Fill in the letter of the dark shape.

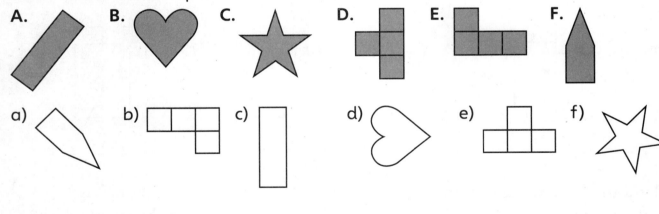

6. Circle the 2 shapes that are congruent.

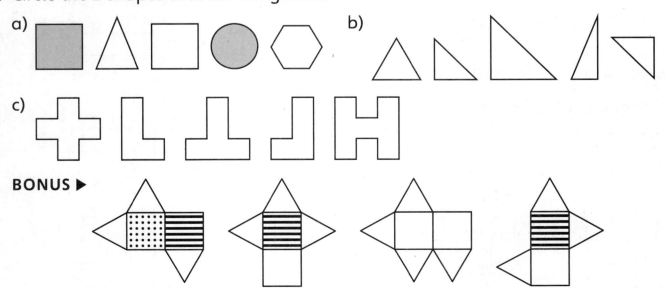

BONUS ▶

7. Draw a shape congruent to the shaded shape.

a)

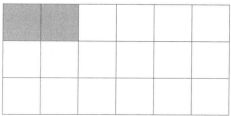

b)

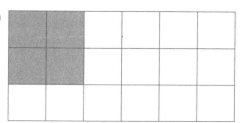

8. Draw a special quadrilateral of the given type that is not congruent to the shaded shape.

a) a square

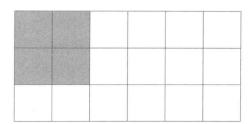

b) a trapezoid

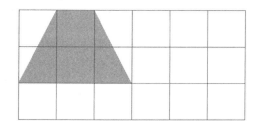

9. Colour the congruent shapes the same colour. You will need 4 different colours.

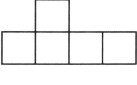
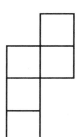
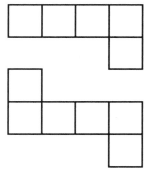
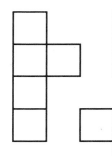
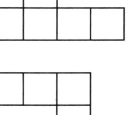

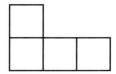
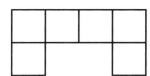

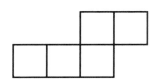

10. Draw 2 triangles that are not congruent.

11. Are the shapes congruent? Explain.

a)

b)

G3-I5 Translations

1. Count the squares to say how many units right the dot slides from *A* to *B*.

a)

_____3_____ units right

b)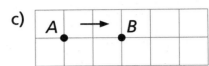

_____ units right

c)

_____ units right

2. Count the squares to say how many units left the dot slides from *A* to *B*.

a)

_____5_____ units left

b)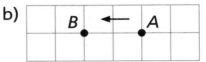

_____ units left

c)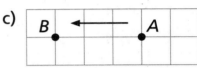

_____ units left

3. Slide the dot.

a) 4 units right

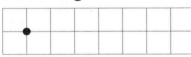

b) 6 units left

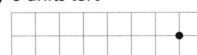

c) 7 units right

4. How many units right and how many units down does the dot slide from *A* to *B*?

a)

_____4_____ units right

_____2_____ units down

b)

_____ units right

_____ units down

c)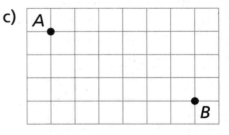

_____ units right

_____ units down

d)

_____ units right

_____ unit down

e)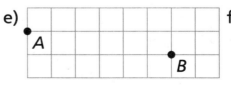

_____ units right

_____ units down

f)

_____ units right

_____ units down

5. Slide the dot.

a) 4 units right, 2 units up b) 5 units left, 3 units up c) 3 units left, 3 units down

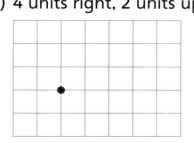 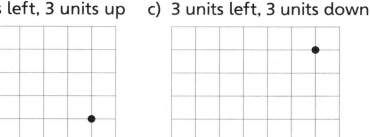

d) 2 units right, I unit down e) I unit left, 2 units down f) 5 units right, 2 units up

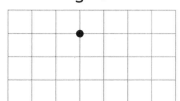 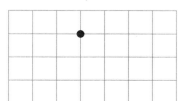 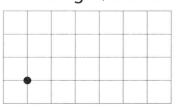

6. Shade the same shape on the second grid. Make sure the dots are on the same vertex of both shapes.

a)   b)   c)

d)   e)   f)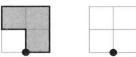

g) 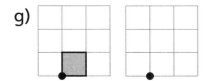 h) 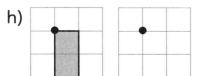 i)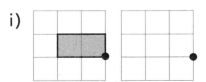

7. Copy the shape so that the dots are on the same vertex of both shapes.

a) 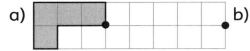 b) 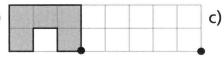 c)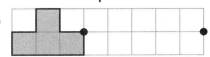

When you slide a shape without turning or flipping it over, you **translate** it.

8. Translate the shape 5 units left. First slide the dot, then copy the shape.

a) 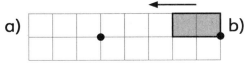 b)  c)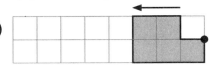

9. Translate the shape. First, draw the arrow to show the direction. Slide the dot, then copy the shape.

a) 3 units right

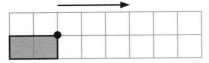

b) 3 units left

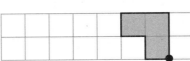

c) 4 units right

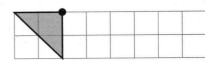

d) 2 units down

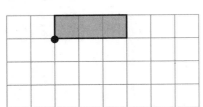

e) 2 units up

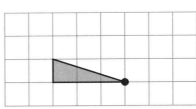

f) 3 units down

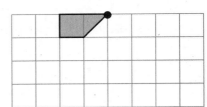

To translate a shape 5 units right and 2 units down:

Step 1: Draw a dot on any vertex of the shape.

Step 2: Draw an arrow the number of units right.

Step 3: Draw an arrow the number of units down from the end of the first arrow. Draw a dot at the end of the arrow.

Step 4: Draw the new shape so that the dots are on the same vertex of both shapes.

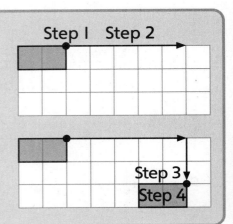

10. Do steps 1, 2, and 3 to translate the shape.

a) 3 units right, 1 unit up

b) 4 units left, 2 units down

c) 3 units left, 2 units up

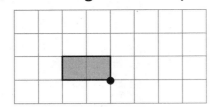
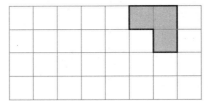

11. Translate the shape.

a) 3 units right, 2 units up

b) 1 unit left, 3 units up

c) 5 units right, 1 unit down

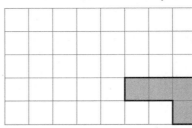
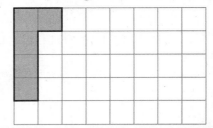

G3-I7 Reflections

I. The dashed line is the mirror line. Finish drawing the mirror image.

a)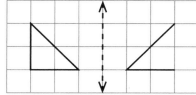

b)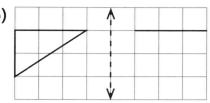

c)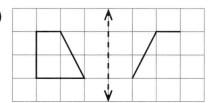

d)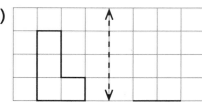

e)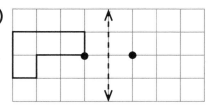

f)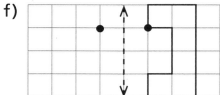

> When you draw a mirror image of a shape, you **reflect** the shape in the mirror line.

2. Reflect the shape in the dashed mirror line.

a)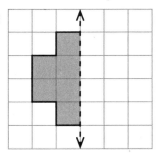

b)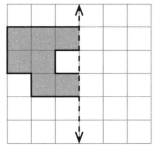

c)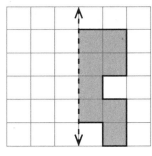

d)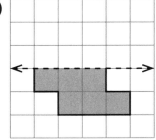

e)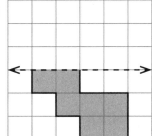

f)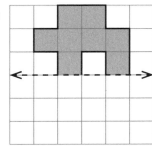

3. a) Draw your own shape on one side of the mirror line. Reflect it in the mirror line.

b) Are the shapes you drew congruent? How do you know?

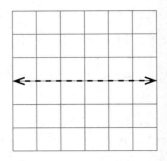

_____

_____

4. Grace makes a pattern by reflecting shapes in vertical lines. Draw the next 3 terms in her pattern.

a)
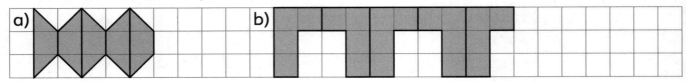

b)
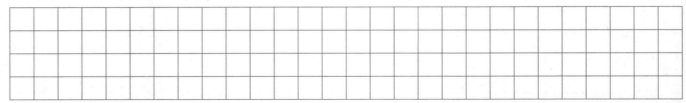

5. Use reflections to draw your own pattern of shapes.

Equal and Not Equal

◯ Add.

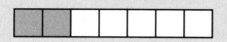

$2 + 5 = \underline{\ 7\ }$

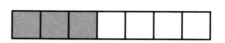

$3 + 4 = \underline{\ \ \ \ }$

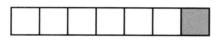

$6 + 1 = \underline{\ \ \ \ }$

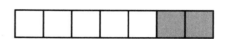

$5 + 2 = \underline{\ \ \ \ }$

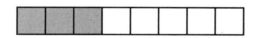

$\underline{\ \ \ \ } = 3 + 5$

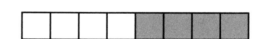

$\underline{\ \ \ \ } = 4 + 4$

$6 + 2 = \underline{\ \ \ \ }$

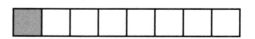

$1 + 7 = \underline{\ \ \ \ }$

$\underline{\ \ \ \ } = 5 + 3$

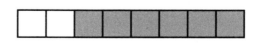

$\underline{\ \ \ \ } = 2 + 6$

☐ Use the model to subtract.

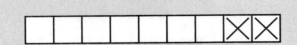

$$9 - 2 = \underline{\;7\;}$$

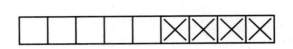

$$9 - 4 = \underline{\quad}$$

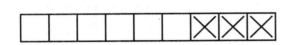

$$9 - 3 = \underline{\quad}$$

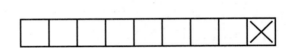

$$\underline{\quad} = 9 - 1$$

☐ Finish the model to subtract.

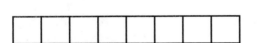

$$8 - 2 = \underline{\quad}$$

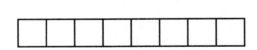

$$8 - 6 = \underline{\quad}$$

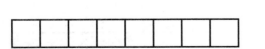

$$\underline{\quad} = 8 - 4$$

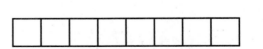

$$\underline{\quad} = 8 - 5$$

☐ Write one sentence for both.

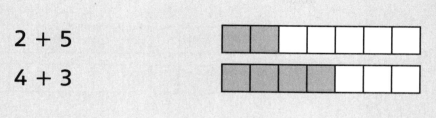

2 + 5

4 + 3

___2 + 5___ = ___4 + 3___

3 + 6

5 + 4

_____ = _____

9 − 3

8 − 2

_____ = _____

7 − 1

9 − 3

_____ = _____

☐ Write **equal** or **not equal**.

7 + 2

4 + 5

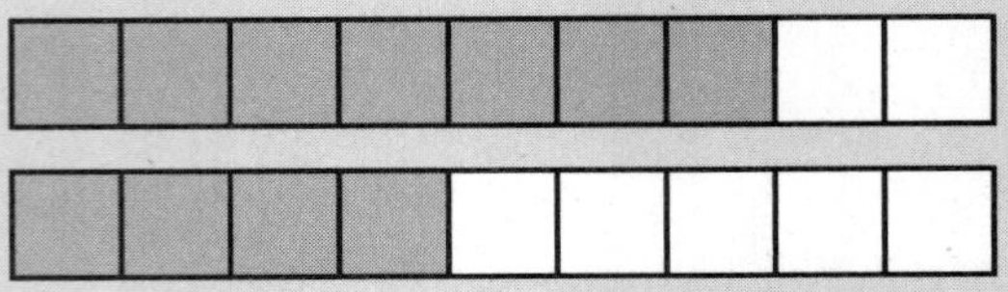

7 + 2 and 4 + 5 are ___equal___.

5 + 6

8 + 4

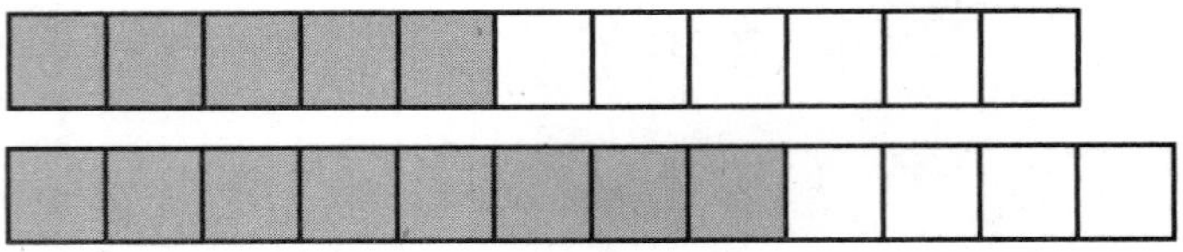

5 + 6 and 8 + 4 are _____.

7 + 3

6 + 4

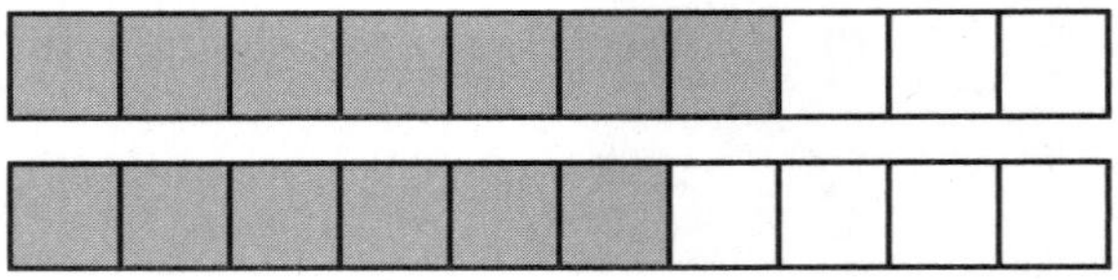

7 + 3 and 6 + 4 are _____.

9 + 2

2 + 8

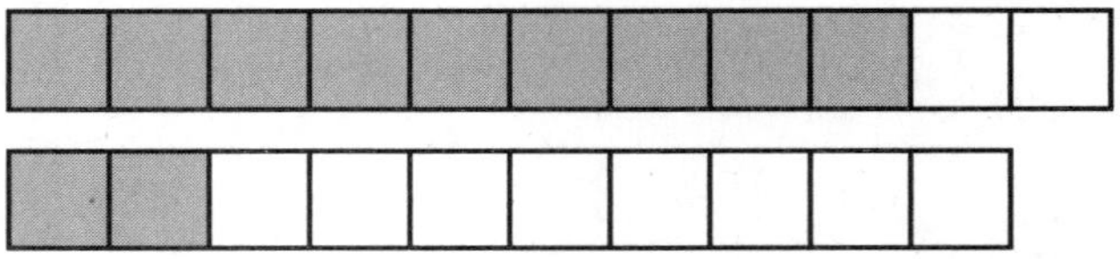

9 + 2 and 2 + 8 are _____.

◯ Write **equal** or **not equal**.

7 − 2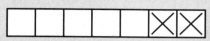

8 − 3

7 − 2 and 8 − 3 are ___equal___.

11 − 3

8 − 1

11 − 3 and 8 − 1 are _____.

9 − 3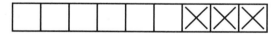

8 − 3

9 − 3 and 8 − 3 are _____.

10 − 5

9 − 4

10 − 5 and 9 − 4 are _____.

Write = for equal. Write ≠ for not equal.

8 − 3

9 − 2

8 − 3 $\boxed{\neq}$ 9 − 2

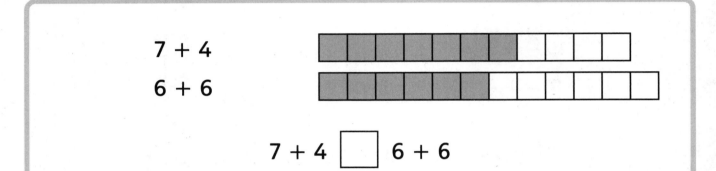

7 + 4

6 + 6

7 + 4 ☐ 6 + 6

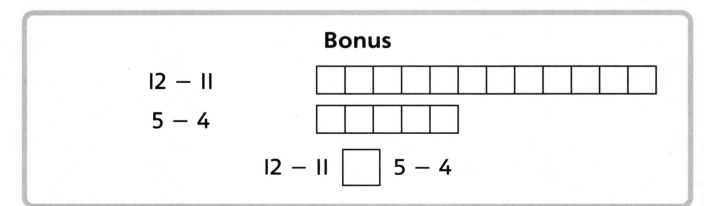

7 + 3

8 + 2

7 + 3 ☐ 8 + 2

Bonus

12 − 11

5 − 4

12 − 11 ☐ 5 − 4

Equality and Inequality with Balances

☐ Add cubes to one side to balance the pans.

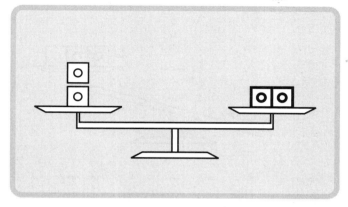

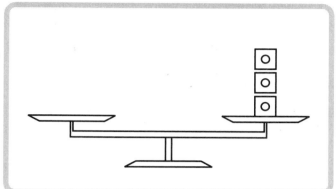

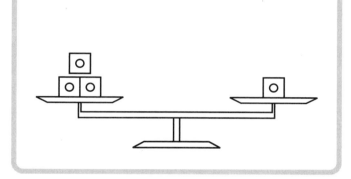

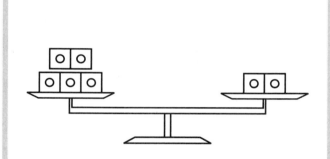

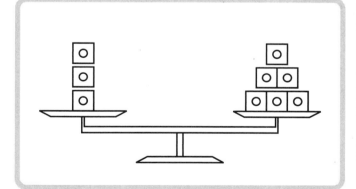

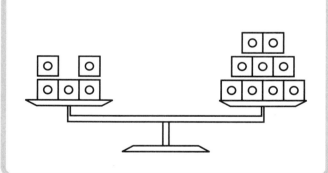

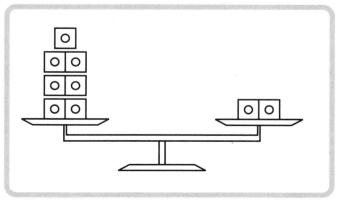

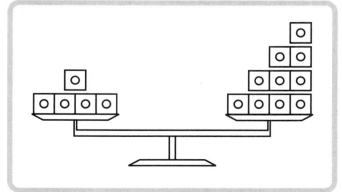

☐ Draw cubes to make the balance correct.

Number Sense 2-29

☐ Add balls to one side to balance the pans.
☐ Write an addition sentence.

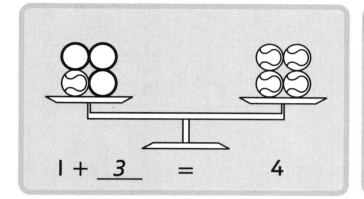

1 + _3_ = 4

2 + ___ = 3

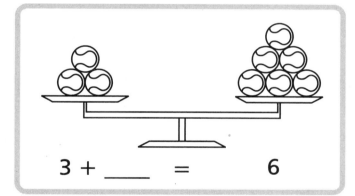

3 + ___ = 6

4 + ___ = 6

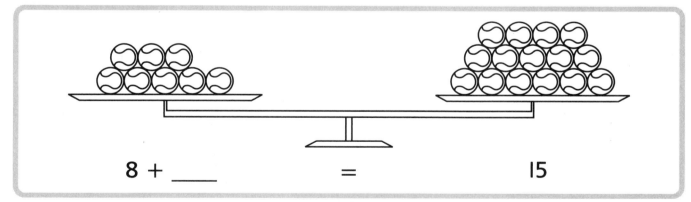

8 + ___ = 15

Bonus

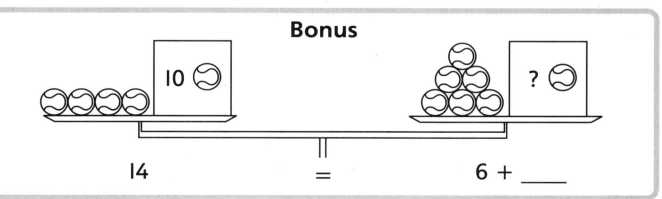

14 = 6 + ___

Remove cubes from one side to balance the pans.

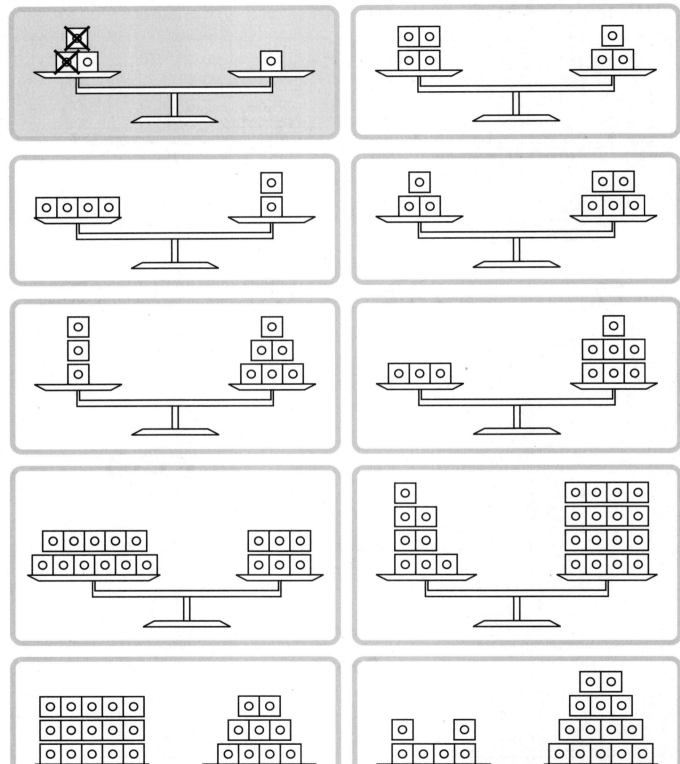

Remove fruits from one side to balance the pans.
Write a subtraction sentence.

6 − _2_ = 4

5 − ___ = 1

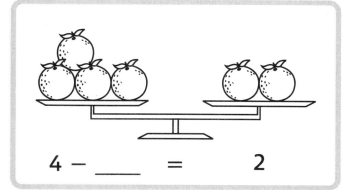

4 − ___ = 2

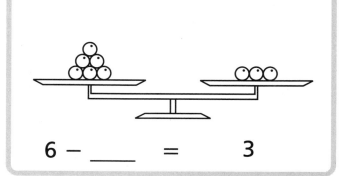

6 − ___ = 3

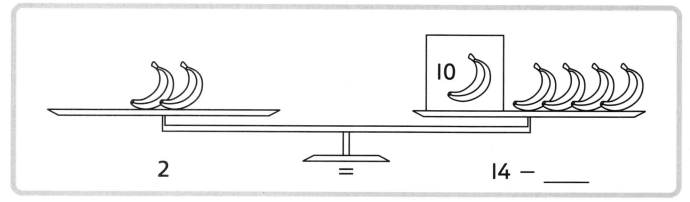

2 = 14 − ___

19 − ___ = 5

Missing Numbers

☐ Find the missing number.

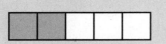

$2 + \underline{\ 3\ } = 5$

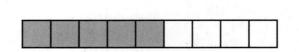

$5 + \underline{} = 9$

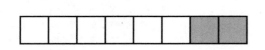

$\underline{} + 2 = 8$

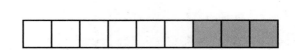

$9 = \underline{} + 3$

☐ Finish the model to find the missing number.

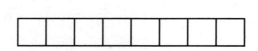

$3 + \underline{} = 8$

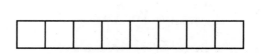

$8 = \underline{} + 4$

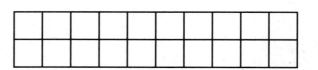

$20 = 11 + \underline{}$

⬜ Find the missing number.

1	2	3	4	X̶5̶	X̶6̶

$$6 - \underline{\ 2\ } = 4$$

1	2	3	4	X̶5̶	X̶6̶	X̶7̶

$$7 - \underline{\quad} = 4$$

1	2	3	4	5	X̶6̶	X̶7̶

$$5 = 7 - \underline{\quad}$$

1	2	3	X̶4̶	X̶5̶	X̶6̶

$$3 = 6 - \underline{\quad}$$

⬜ Finish the model to find the missing number.

1	2	3	4	5	6	7	8

$$8 - \underline{\quad} = 3$$

1	2	3	4	5	6	7	8

$$6 = 8 - \underline{\quad}$$

1	2	3	4	5	6	7	8	9	10
11	12	13	14	15	16	17	18	19	20

$$20 - \underline{\quad} = 7$$

☐ Finish the model to find the missing number.

1	2	3	4	5	6	7	8	9	10
11	12	13	14	15	16				

$$16 = \underline{} + 7$$

1	2	3	4	5	6	7	8	9	10
11	12	13	14	15	16	17	18		

$$9 + \underline{} = 18$$

1	2	3	4	5	6	7	8	9	10
11	12	13	14	15					

$$15 = 8 + \underline{}$$

1	2	3	4	5	6	7	8	9	10
11	12	13	14	15	16	17			

$$17 = \underline{} + 7$$

☐ Finish the model to find the missing number.

1	2	3	4	5	6	7	✗	✗	✗
✗	✗	✗	✗	✗	✗				

$$16 - \underline{} = 7$$

1	2	3	4	5	6	7	8	9	10
11	12	13	14	15	16	17	18		

$$10 = 18 - \underline{}$$

1	2	3	4	5	6	7	8	9	10
11	12	13	14						

$$8 = 14 - \underline{}$$

1	2	3	4	5	6	7	8	9	10
11	12	13	14	15	16	17			

$$17 - \underline{} = 9$$

◯ Finish the model to find the missing number.

1	2	3	4	5	6	7	X̶	X̶	X̶
X̶	X̶	X̶	X̶	X̶	X̶	X̶			

$$17 - \underline{} = 7$$

1	2	3	4	5	6	7	8	9	10
11	12	13	14	15	16	17	18	19	

$$19 = 9 + \underline{}$$

1	2	3	4	5	6	7	8	9	10
11	12	13							

$$\underline{} + 6 = 13$$

Bonus

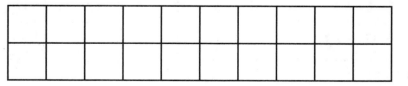

$$2 = 19 - \underline{}$$

Comparing Number Sentences

⬜ Write two subtraction sentences.
⬜ Circle the totals.

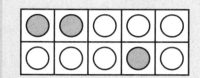

⑩ − __3__ = __7__
⑩ − __7__ = __3__

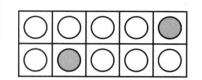

10 − __2__ = ____
10 − __8__ = ____

10 − ____ = ____
10 − ____ = ____

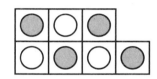

__7__ − ____ = ____
__7__ − ____ = ____

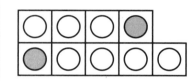

____ − ____ = ____
____ − ____ = ____

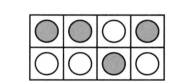

____ − ____ = ____
____ − ____ = ____

⬜ Write two addition sentences.
⬜ Write two subtraction sentences.
⬜ Circle the totals.

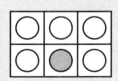

__1__ + __5__ = ⑥
__5__ + __1__ = ⑥
⑥ − __5__ = __1__
⑥ − __1__ = __5__

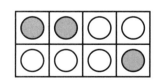

____ + ____ = ____
____ + ____ = ____
____ − ____ = ____
____ − ____ = ____

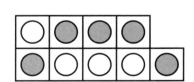

____ + ____ = ____
____ + ____ = ____
____ − ____ = ____
____ − ____ = ____

☐ Circle the total.
☐ Write two subtraction sentences for the addition.

3 + 7 = ⑩	2 + 5 = ⑦	3 + 6 = ⑨
10 − 3 = 7	7 − 2 = 5	_____
10 − 7 = 3	_____	_____

9 + 2 = 11	12 = 5 + 7	13 = 4 + 9
_____	_____	_____
_____	_____	_____

☐ Circle the total.
☐ Write two addition sentences for the subtraction.

⑧ − 3 = 5	⑫ − 4 = 8	⑦ − 3 = 4
3 + 5 = 8	4 + 8 = 12	_____
5 + 3 = 8	_____	_____

11 − 6 = 5	7 = 9 − 2	8 = 15 − 7
_____	_____	_____
_____	_____	_____

◯ Write four number sentences for each picture.

$4 + 3 = 7$ $3 + 4 = 7$

$7 - 3 = 4$ $7 - 4 = 3$

_____   _____

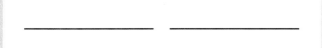

_____   _____

_____   _____

_____   _____

_____   _____

_____   _____

	2		☐		4	
+	4		☐	+	2	
	6		☐		6	
			☐			
	6		☐		6	
−	4		☐	−	2	
	2		☐		4	

More and Fewer

☐ Draw ◯ or △ to show which is fewer.

	Fewer ◯ or △?
◯ ◯ ◯ ◯ ◯ ◯ △ △ △ △	△
◯ ◯ △ △ △ △ △	
△ △ △ △ △ △ △ ◯ ◯ ◯	
△ △ △ △ ◯ ◯ ◯ ◯ ◯ ◯ ◯	

☐ Circle **more** or **fewer** △.

	More or fewer △?
◯ ◯ ◯ △ △ △ △ △ △	(more) fewer
◯ ◯ ◯ ◯ △ △	more fewer
△ △ △ △ △ ◯ ◯ ◯ ◯ ◯ ◯ ◯ ◯	more fewer
△ △ △ △ △ △ △ △ ◯ ◯ ◯ ◯ ◯ ◯	more fewer

☐ Draw ◯ or △ to show which is fewer.
☐ Write how many fewer.

	Fewer ◯ or △?	How many fewer?
◯◯◯ △△△△△	◯	2
◯◯◯◯◯◯ △△		
△△△△ ◯◯◯◯◯◯		
△△△△△△△△△ ◯◯◯◯		

☐ Draw ◯ or △ to show which is more.
☐ Find how many more.

	More ◯ or △?	How many more?
5◯ and 8△	△	_8_ – _5_ = _3_
12◯ and 7△		____ – ____ = ____
14◯ and 12△		____ – ____ = ____
9◯ and 12△		____ – ____ = ____
11◯ and 6△		____ – ____ = ____
10◯ and 15△		____ – ____ = ____

☐ Underline who has fewer.
☐ Find how many fewer.

	How many fewer?
<u>Tess</u> has 5 shells. Jack has 8 shells.	_8_ − _5_ = _3_
Emma has 17 shells. Fred has 7 shells.	____ − ____ = ____
Ray has 14 shells. Grace has 18 shells.	____ − ____ = ____
Ava has 9 shells. Ken has 15 shells.	____ − ____ = ____
Nina has 11 shells. Ivan has 4 shells.	____ − ____ = ____

☐ Find how many more or fewer.

Yu has 8 raisins. Bill has 12 raisins.

How many more raisins does Bill have? ___ − ___ = ___

Alex has 13 raisins. Ethan has 2 raisins.

How many fewer raisins does Ethan have? ___ − ___ = ___

Clara has 13 raisins. Amir has 2 raisins.

How many more raisins does Clara have? ___ − ___ = ___

Compare Using Pictures

☐ Circle who has more. Underline who has fewer.
☐ Draw triangles for Kim.

⬭Kim⬭ has 3 more △ than <u>Sam</u>.

Sam	△	△	△	△	△			
Kim	△	△	△	△	△	△	△	△

Kim has 3 fewer △ than Sam.

Sam	△	△	△	△	△			
Kim								

Kim has 1 more △ than Sam.

Sam	△	△	△	△	△			
Kim								

Kim has 2 more △ than Sam.

Sam	△	△	△	△	△			
Kim								

Kim has 4 fewer △ than Sam.

Sam	△	△	△	△	△			
Kim								

☐ Draw triangles for Tess.
☐ Circle how many triangles Tess has.

| Glen has 5 △. | △ △ △ △ △ | $(5 + 2)$ |
| Tess has 2 more △ than Glen. | △ △ △ △ △ △ △ | $5 - 2$ |

| Glen has 3 △. | △ △ △ | $3 + 2$ |
| Tess has 2 fewer △ than Glen. | | $3 - 2$ |

| Glen has 6 △. | △ △ △ △ △ △ | $6 + 3$ |
| Tess has 3 more △ than Glen. | | $6 - 3$ |

| Glen has 4 △. | △ △ △ △ | $4 + 3$ |
| Tess has 3 fewer △ than Glen. | | $4 - 3$ |

| Glen has 7 △. | △ △ △ △ △ △ △ | $7 + 1$ |
| Tess has 1 fewer △ than Glen. | | $7 - 1$ |

Comparing and Word Problems (I)

☐ Circle which is more. Underline which is fewer.
☐ Find how many circles.

△		How many ◯?
5	There are 3 more ⬭(◯) than △.	_5 + 3_ = _8_
6	There are 3 fewer <u>◯</u> than ⬭(△).	_6 −_ ___ = ___
4	There are 2 more ◯ than △.	_____ = ___
9	There are 6 fewer ◯ than △.	_____ = ___
15	There are 4 fewer ◯ than △.	_____ = ___
13	There are 5 fewer ◯ than △.	_____ = ___
9	There are 4 more ◯ than △.	_____ = ___
21	There are 5 more ◯ than △.	_____ = ___
27	There are 3 fewer ◯ than △.	_____ = ___
39	There are 6 fewer ◯ than △.	_____ = ___

☐ Circle which is more. Underline which is fewer.
☐ Add or subtract.

Mona has 25 apples.

She has 8 more (pears) than <u>apples</u>.

How many pears does Mona have?

$\underline{\quad 25 + 8 = \quad\quad\quad}$

Marko has 46 red flowers.

He has 7 fewer <u>yellow</u> flowers than (red) flowers.

How many yellow flowers does Marko have?

_____

Tom has 93 blocks.

He has 6 fewer toy cars than blocks.

How many toy cars does Tom have?

_____

Lynn drew 28 circles.

She drew 9 more triangles than circles.

How many triangles did Lynn draw?

_____

Comparing and Word Problems (2)

☐ Underline **more** or **fewer**.

Maria has 3 more stickers than Ben.
Ben has more / <u>fewer</u> stickers than Maria.

Maria has 3 fewer stickers than Ben.
Ben has more / fewer stickers than Maria.

Carl has 2 more stickers than Jen.
Jen has more / fewer stickers than Carl.

Carl has 2 fewer stickers than Jen.
Jen has more / fewer stickers than Carl.

☐ Circle who has more. Underline who has fewer.
☐ Draw triangles for Rani.

(Kyle) has 2 more △ than <u>Rani</u>.

Kyle	△	△	△	△	△		
Rani	△	△	△				

Kyle has 2 fewer △ than Rani.

Kyle	△	△	△	△	△		
Rani							

Kyle has 3 more △ than Rani.

Kyle	△	△	△	△	△		
Rani							

Liz has 10 grapes.

☐ Circle who has more grapes. Underline who has fewer grapes.
☐ Fill in the table.

	Does Jon have more or fewer?	How many does Jon have?
(Liz) has 2 more grapes than <u>Jon</u>.	*fewer*	10 ⊖ 2
Liz has 2 fewer grapes than Jon.		10 ◯ 2
Liz has 3 more grapes than Jon.		10 ◯ 3
Liz has 3 fewer grapes than Jon.		10 ◯ 3

☐ Circle who has more. Underline who has fewer.
☐ Fill in the table.

	Does Don have more or fewer?	How many does Don have?
Amy has 8 grapes. <u>Amy</u> has 3 fewer grapes than (Don)	*more*	$8 + 3$ = *11*
Amy has 8 grapes. Amy has 3 more grapes than Don.		_____ = ____
Amy has 6 grapes. Amy has 5 fewer grapes than Don.		_____ = ____
Amy has 11 grapes. Amy has 7 more grapes than Don.		_____ = ____

☐ Circle who has more pencils. Underline who has fewer pencils.
☐ Find how many pencils David has.

Hanna has 26 pencils.

Hanna has 3 fewer pencils than (David)

How many pencils does David have?   26 + 3 = _____

Hanna has 43 pencils.

(Hanna) has 10 more pencils than David.

How many pencils does David have?   _____

Hanna has 26 pencils.

Hanna has 7 fewer pencils than David.

How many pencils does David have?   _____

Hanna has 65 pencils.

Hanna has 8 more pencils than David.

How many pencils does David have?   _____

Hanna has 79 pencils.

Hanna has 9 more pencils than David.

How many pencils does David have?   _____

Subtracting in Word Problems

☐ Subtract by counting forwards.
☐ Write a sentence to describe how many **more**.

Sara has 12 marbles.
Ray has 8 marbles.

Sara has 4 more marbles than Ray.

Sara has 7 apples.
Sara has 9 oranges.

_____

Ray has 8 crayons.
Ray has 5 markers.

_____

Sara has 6 crayons.
Ray has 10 crayons.

_____

☐ Circle the correct way to answer the question.
☐ Write the answer.

Kate had five bananas.
She ate three bananas.

$5 + 3$ $\boxed{5 - 3}$

How many bananas are **left**? __2__

There are eight big pencils.
There are five little pencils.

$8 + 5$ $8 - 5$

How many pencils **altogether**? _____

There are eight big pencils.
There are five little pencils.

$8 + 5$ $8 - 5$

How many **more** big pencils **than** little pencils? _____

There are fourteen red balloons.
There are three blue balloons.

$14 + 3$ $14 - 3$

How many **more** red balloons **than** blue balloons? _____

There are fourteen red balloons.
There are three blue balloons.

$14 + 3$ $14 - 3$

How many balloons **in total**? _____

Cathy has eleven crayons.
Seven of them are red.

$11 + 7$ $11 - 7$

How many are **not** red? _____

More Missing Numbers

⬜ Find the missing number by adding.

4 + 3 = _____   so   _____ − 3 = 4

3 + 2 = _____   so   _____ − 2 = 3

5 + 2 = _____   so   _____ − 2 = 5

_____ − 2 = 4   _____ − 5 = 3   _____ − 3 = 6

⬜ Find the missing number.

<u>31</u> − 4 = 27

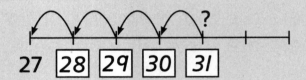

27 28 29 30 31

_____ − 3 = 38

38 ☐ ☐ ☐

_____ − 5 = 49

49

_____ − 2 = 58   _____ − 3 = 47   _____ − 5 = 28

☐ Find the missing number by counting forwards.

27 + 4 = __31__	36 + 3 = ____	2 + 25 = ____
so	so	so
__31__ − 4 = 27	____ − 3 = 36	____ − 25 = 2

____ − 13 = 6	____ − 5 = 21	____ − 4 = 37

☐ Find the missing number by using a picture.

1	2	3	4	5	6̶	7̶	8̶	9̶

__9__ − 4 = 5

1	2	3	4	5	6	7̶	8̶

____ − 2 = 6

1	2	3	4	5̶	6̶	7̶

____ − 3 = 4

1	2	3̶	4̶	5̶	6̶

6 − ____ = 2

☐ Find the missing number by using a number line.

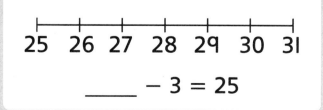

____ − 3 = 25

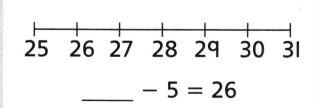

____ − 5 = 26

☐ Find the missing number in ____ − 26 = 5.
Explain how you found it.

Missing Numbers in Word Problems

⬜ Write the number sentence for the story.

There are red marbles.

There are 5 blue marbles.

There are 9 marbles altogether.

$$\begin{array}{r} \blacksquare \\ +\ \ 5 \\ \hline 9 \end{array}$$

There are 7 red marbles.

There are 3 blue marbles.

There are marbles altogether.

There are 4 red marbles.

There are blue marbles.

There are 6 marbles altogether.

There are 5 red marbles.

There are blue marbles.

There are 8 marbles altogether.

There are red marbles.

There are 2 blue marbles.

There are 7 marbles altogether.

Write the number sentence for the story.

There are ☐ children at the park.
There are 3 adults at the park.
There are 8 people altogether.

$$\begin{array}{r} \boxed{} \\ +\quad 3 \\ \hline 8 \end{array}$$

There are 3 glasses of milk.
There are 8 glasses of juice.
There are ☐ glasses altogether.

Luc has 4 stickers.
Tristan has ☐ stickers.
Together, they have 9 stickers.

Tasha has ☐ hockey cards.
Tasha has 2 baseball cards.
Tasha has 7 cards altogether.

4 children were playing soccer.
3 more joined them.
Then there were ☐ children playing.

Fill in the missing numbers.

◯ Write the number sentence for the story.

There were ☐ flies.
The frog ate 3 of them.
There are 6 flies left.

$$\begin{array}{r} \blacksquare \\ -\ \ 3 \\ \hline 6 \end{array}$$

There were 8 flies.
The frog ate ☐ of them.
There are 5 flies left.

There were 7 flies.
The frog ate 4 of them.
There are ☐ flies left.

There were 9 flies.
The frog ate ☐ of them.
There are 4 flies left.

There were ☐ flies.
The frog ate 2 of them.
There are 5 flies left.

☐ Write the number sentence for the story.

There were ☐ children playing.
3 of them went home.
There are 5 children still playing.

$$\begin{array}{r} \boxed{} \\ -\quad 3 \\ \hline 5 \end{array}$$

There are 7 marbles.
4 of them are red.
☐ marbles are not red.

Jayden has 8 cousins.
☐ cousins live outside of Canada.
3 cousins live in Canada.

Jayden has 8 cousins.
3 cousins live in Canada.
☐ cousins live outside of Canada.

Luc had ☐ stickers.
He gave 2 away.
He has 6 left.

☐ Fill in the missing numbers.

☐ Match the number sentence to the story.
☐ Fill in the missing number.

There were 8 carrots.
Kim ate ■ of them.
There are 5 carrots left.

$7 - 5 = \boxed{}$

Anton ate ■ carrots.
Josh ate 2 carrots.
Together, they ate 6 carrots.

$8 - \boxed{} = 5$

There were ■ carrots.
Raydar ate 3 of them.
There are 4 carrots left.

$3 + \boxed{} = 6$

There were 7 carrots.
Lynn ate 5 of them.
There are ■ left.

$\boxed{} + 2 = 6$

Luc ate 3 carrots.
Lynn ate ■ carrots.
Together, they ate 6 carrots.

$\boxed{} - 3 = 4$

Making 10

☐ Hold up the correct number of fingers.

How many fingers are not up?

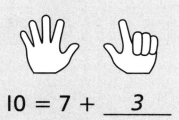

$10 = 7 + \underline{\ \ 3\ \ }$

$10 = 3 + \underline{\ \ \ \ \ }$

$10 = 4 + \underline{\ \ \ \ \ }$

$10 = 5 + \underline{\ \ \ \ \ }$

$$\begin{array}{r} 9 \\ + \ \square \\ \hline 10 \end{array}$$

$$\begin{array}{r} 1 \\ + \ \square \\ \hline 10 \end{array}$$

$$\begin{array}{r} 2 \\ + \ \square \\ \hline 10 \end{array}$$

$$\begin{array}{r} 10 \\ + \ \square \\ \hline 10 \end{array}$$

$10 - 8 = \underline{\ \ \ \ \ }$

$10 - 6 = \underline{\ \ \ \ \ }$

$10 - 5 = \underline{\ \ \ \ \ }$

$10 - 9 = \underline{\ \ \ \ \ }$

○ Circle the number that makes 10 with the number in the box.

8	1 ②3 4 5
6	1 2 3 4 5
7	1 2 3 4 5
5	1 2 3 4 5
9	1 2 3 4 5

4	6 9 7 8
1	6 9 7 8
3	6 9 7 8
2	9 6 8 5 7 4

○ Circle the two numbers that make 10.

4 5 6	3 7 9	4 5 5
1 2 3 9	4 5 6 7	2 4 6 9
1 9 3 5	2 4 3 8	2 3 7 9
1 2 6 7 8	2 3 4 7 9	1 3 4 8 9
2 3 6 8 9	2 3 4 5 6	3 5 6 7 8

◯ Write the missing numbers.

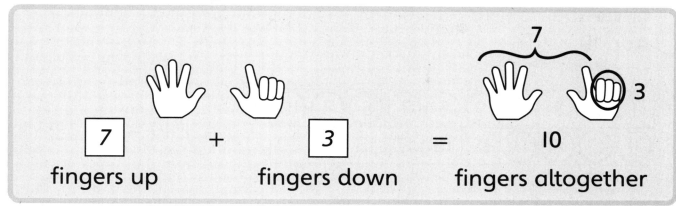

| **7** | + | **3** | = | 10 |
| fingers up | | fingers down | | fingers altogether |

| ☐ | + | ☐ | = | 10 |
| fingers up | | finger down | | fingers altogether |

| ☐ | + | ☐ | = | 10 |
| fingers up | | fingers down | | fingers altogether |

| ☐ | + | ☐ | = | 10 |
| fingers up | | fingers down | | fingers altogether |

Adding 10 and Subtracting 10

☐ Circle the next 10 numbers.
☐ Add 10.

1	2	3	**4**	⑤	⑥	⑦	⑧	⑨	⑩
⑪	⑫	⑬	⑭	15	16	17	18	19	20

$4 + 10 = $ _____

11	12	13	14	15	16	17	18	**19**	20
21	22	23	24	25	26	27	28	29	30

$19 + 10 = $ _____

31	32	33	34	35	36	37	**38**	39	40
41	42	43	44	45	46	47	48	49	50

$38 + 10 = $ _____

81	82	83	84	85	86	87	88	89	**90**
91	92	93	94	95	96	97	98	99	100

$90 + 10 = $ _____

☐ Add 10 by moving down a row.

1	2	**3**	4	5	6	**7**	8	**9**	10
11	12	13	14	15	16	17	18	19	20

$3 + 10 = $ _____

$7 + 10 = $ _____

$9 + 10 = $ _____

182

Number Sense 2-40

☐ Move down a row to add 10.

1	2	3	4	5	6	7	8	9	10
11	12	13	14	15	16	17	18	19	20
21	22	23	24	25	26	27	28	29	30
31	32	33	34	35	36	37	38	39	40

2 + 10 = _____   8 + 10 = _____   20 + 10 = _____

17 + 10 = _____   25 + 10 = _____   19 + 10 = _____

11 + 10 = _____   23 + 10 = _____   30 + 10 = _____

What comes out of the adding 10 machine?

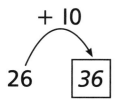
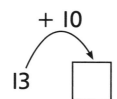
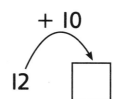
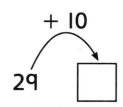

When adding 10, the _____ digit stays the same
ones/tens

and the _____ digit goes up by 1.
ones/tens

☐ Add 10.

64 + 10 = _____   55 + 10 = _____   87 + 10 = _____

◻ Circle the previous 10 numbers.
◻ Subtract 10.

1	2	3	4	5	6	⑦	⑧	⑨	⑩
⑪	⑫	⑬	⑭	⑮	⑯	17	18	19	20

$17 - 10 =$ _____

11	12	13	14	15	16	17	18	19	20
21	22	23	24	25	26	27	28	29	30

$30 - 10 =$ _____

41	42	43	44	45	46	47	48	49	50
51	52	53	54	55	56	57	58	59	60

$52 - 10 =$ _____

◻ Move up a row to subtract 10.

71	72	73	74	75	76	77	78	79	80
81	82	83	84	85	86	87	88	89	90

$82 - 10 =$ _____

$85 - 10 =$ _____

$90 - 10 =$ _____

When subtracting 10, the _____ digit stays the same
ones/tens

and the _____ digit goes _____ by 1.
ones/tens   up/down

◻ Subtract 10.

$76 - 10 =$ _____ $38 - 10 =$ _____ $99 - 10 =$ _____

☐ Add 10 by adding a tens block.

25 + 10 = ___35___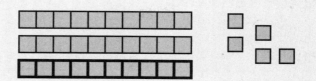

17 + 10 = _____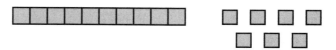

20 + 10 = _____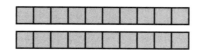

11 + 10 = _____   46 + 10 = _____   39 + 10 = _____

☐ Subtract 10 by taking away a tens block.

26 − 10 = ___16___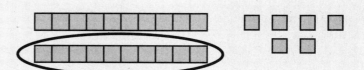

17 − 10 = _____

23 − 10 = _____

18 − 10 = _____   29 − 10 = _____   32 − 10 = _____

Adding and Subtracting 10 Mentally

☐ Write the tens digit.

42 + 10 = __ 2   37 + 10 = __ 7   16 + 10 = __ 6

73 + 10 = __ 3   56 + 10 = __ 6   45 + 10 = __ 5

☐ Write the ones digit.

24 + 10 = _3_ __   62 + 10 = _7_ __   28 + 10 = _3_ __

40 + 10 = _5_ __   66 + 10 = _7_ __   53 + 10 = _6_ __

☐ Write the missing digit.

13 + 10 = __ 3   87 + 10 = __ 7   68 + 10 = _7_ __

47 + 10 = _5_ __   32 + 10 = __ 2   75 + 10 = _8_ __

☐ Add 10.

43 + 10 = _5_ _3_   7 + 10 = __ __   18 + 10 = __ __

32 + 10 = __ __   25 + 10 = __ __   4 + 10 = __ __

60 + 10 = __ __   55 + 10 = __ __   9 + 10 = __ __

☐ Write the tens digit.

42 − 10 = __ 2	37 − 10 = __ 7	26 − 10 = __ 6
50 − 10 = __ 0	78 − 10 = __ 8	45 − 10 = __ 5

☐ Write the ones digit.

24 − 10 = 1 4	34 − 10 = 2 __	29 − 10 = 1 __
28 − 10 = 1 __	54 − 10 = 4 __	76 − 10 = 6 __

☐ Write the missing digit.

74 − 10 = __ 4	36 − 10 = __ 6	28 − 10 = 1 __
87 − 10 = 7 __	68 − 10 = __ 8	47 − 10 = 3 __

☐ Subtract 10.

41 − 10 = 3 1	27 − 10 = __ __	38 − 10 = __ __
18 − 10 = __ __	80 − 10 = __ __	16 − 10 = __ __
54 − 10 = __ __	31 − 10 = __ __	42 − 10 = __ __

☐ Circle the two numbers that make 10.
☐ Add.

⑧ + ② + 5 = 10 + __5__

= __15__

4 + 6 + 7 = 10 + _____

= _____

2 + 3 + 7 = 10 + _____

= _____

1 + 6 + 4 = 10 + _____

= _____

8 + 5 + 5 = 10 + _____

= _____

7 + 6 + 3 = 10 + _____

= _____

4 + 9 + 1 = 10 + _____

= _____

8 + 3 + 2 = 10 + _____

= _____

4 + 5 + 5 = 10 + _____

= _____

2 + 9 + 8 = 10 + _____

= _____

3 + 5 + 7 = 10 + _____

= _____

1 + 8 + 9 = 10 + _____

= _____

Hundreds Chart Pieces

The boxes are pieces from a hundreds chart.

1	2	3	4	5	6	7	8	9	10
11	12	13	14	15	16	17	18	19	20

☐ Find the missing numbers.

Add 1.

3 ☐   17 ☐   19 ☐   6 ☐

Add 10.

23   30   6   24   31   29

Add 1 or 10.

45   50   41   52   53   56

Add 1 then 10, or add 10 then 1.

71   77   74   86   82

☐ Have a partner check your answers using a hundreds chart.

◯ Find the missing numbers.

Subtract 1 or 10.

| | 48 |

| 57 | (below) |

| | 43 |

| 43 | (below) |

| 41 | (below) |

| | 40 |

Subtract 1 then 10, or subtract 10 then 1.

| | | 92 (bottom right) |

| | 89 (bottom right) |

| | | 77 (bottom right) |

| | 85 (bottom right) |

| | 90 (bottom right) |

Add or subtract 1 or 10.

| | 26 |

| 37 | (below) |

| | 39 |

| 39 | |

| 39 | (below) |

Add, subtract, or do both.

| | 18 (below) |

| 24 | |

| | 17 (below) |

| | 15 |

| 35 | 19 |

| | 46 |

| 18 | |

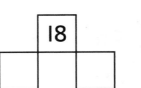

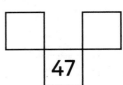

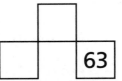

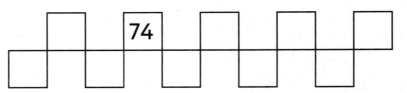

⬜ Write the missing numbers on the hundreds chart pieces.

33		35		37
	44	45	46	47
53	54		56	

11	12	13	
21		23	24
	32	33	

61	62	
71		73
		83
91	92	

64		66
	75	
	85	
94		96

		49
58		
		69
78		

46				50
	57		59	
		68		
	77		79	
86				90

	57	58	59	60
66				
	77			
		88		
			99	100

Comparing Units of Length

☐ Measure two ways.
☐ Write which way needed more units and why.

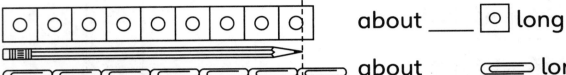

about ____ 🔲 long

about ____ ⬭ long

I used _____ *more / fewer* 🔲 than ⬭
because a 🔲 is _____ *longer / shorter* than a ⬭.

about ____ ▭ long

about ____ ⬛ long

I used _____ ▭ than ⬛
because a ▭ is _____ than a ⬛.

about ____ ⚷ long

about ____ ⬭ long

_____

_____

When You Do Not Have Many Units

☐ Measure a desk two ways.

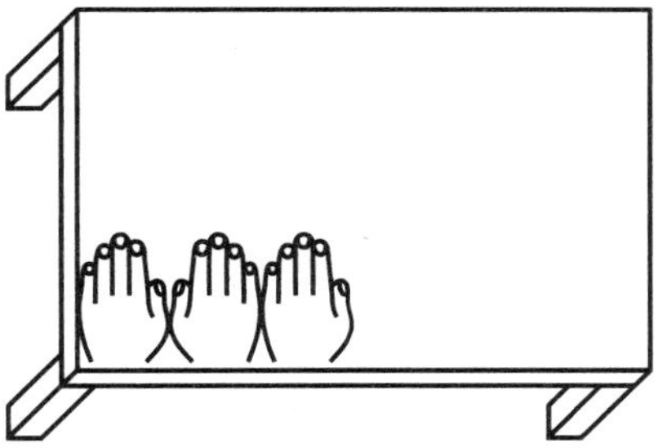

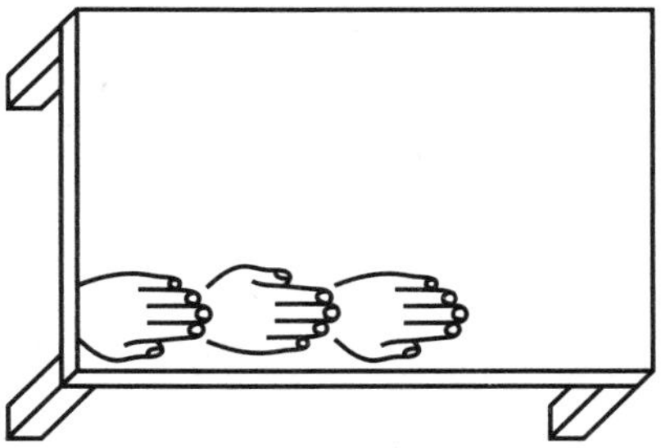

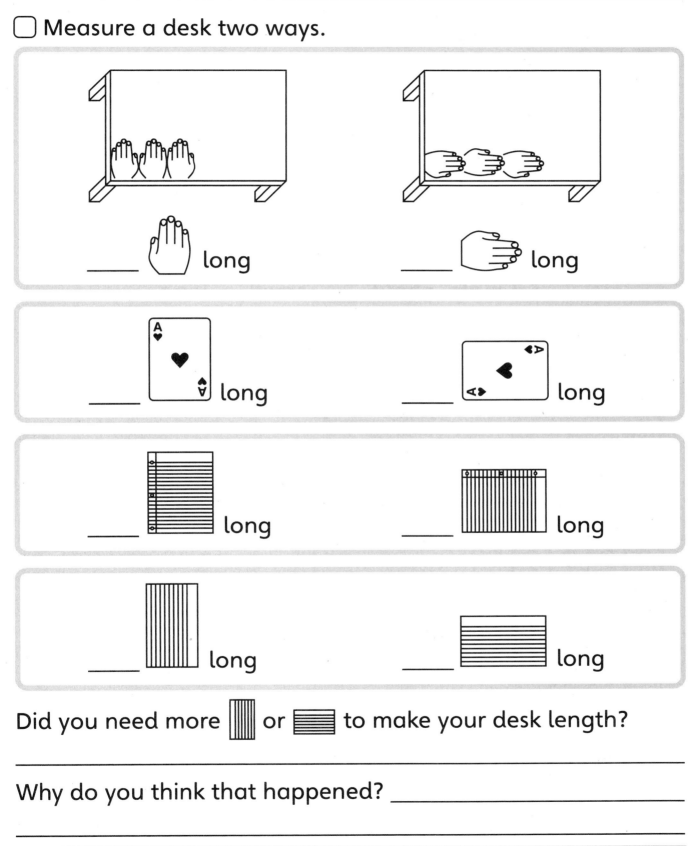

____  long

____  long

____  long

____ 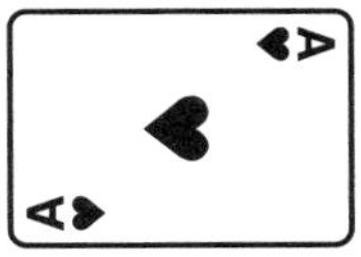 long

____ 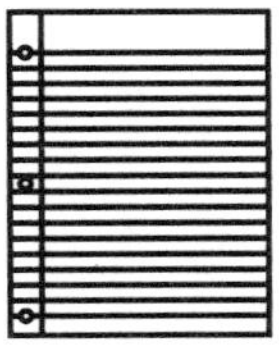 long

____  long

____  long

____  long

Did you need more  or  to make your desk length?

____

Why do you think that happened? ______________________________

____

Estimating

☐ Estimate how many small 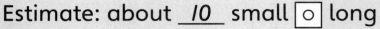.
☐ Check by measuring.

Estimate: about __10__ small ⊡ long

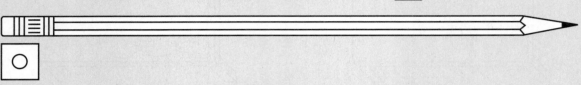

Check: about __15__ small ⊡ long

Estimate: about _____ small ⊡ long

Check: about _____ small ⊡ long

Estimate: about _____ small ⊡ long

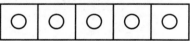

Check: about _____ small ⊡ long

Estimate: about _____ small ⊡ long

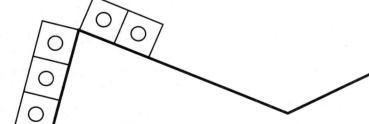

Check: about _____ small ⊡ long

☐ Use pictures to estimate.
☐ Use 🖊 and 🎲 to measure.

Estimate: _____ big ⬭ long
Measure: _____ big ⬭ long

Estimate: _____ small ⬭ long
Measure: _____ small ⬭ long
Estimate: _____ small ☐ long
Measure: _____ small ☐ long

How did knowing the lengths in big 🎲 help you estimate?

_____

_____

Creating Rulers

☐ Make marks with equal spaces between them.
☐ Write the missing numbers on the ruler.

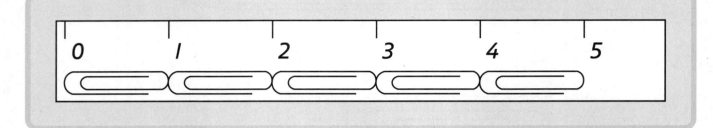

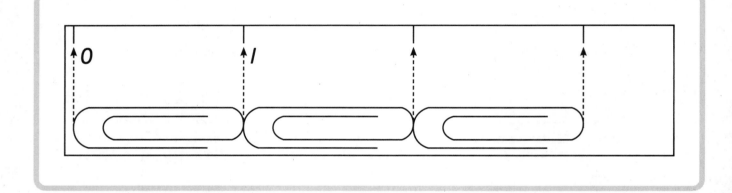

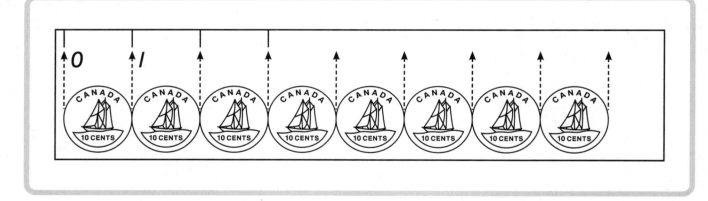

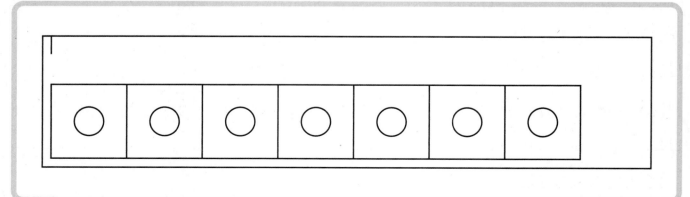

Measurement 2-11

◻ Write how many units long.

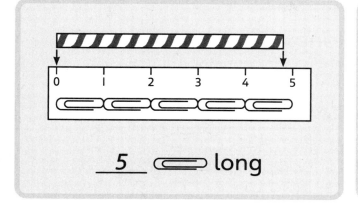

___5___ ⬭ long

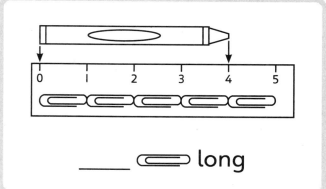

_____ ⬭ long

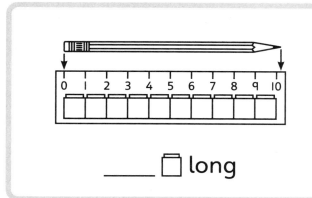

_____ ▢ long

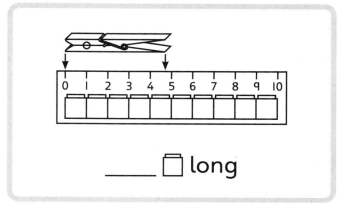

_____ ▢ long

◻ Measure two ways.

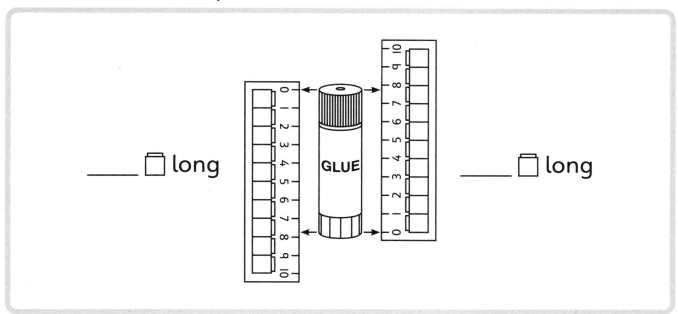

_____ ▢ long

_____ ▢ long

◻ Did you get the same answer? Explain.

Centimetres

A small 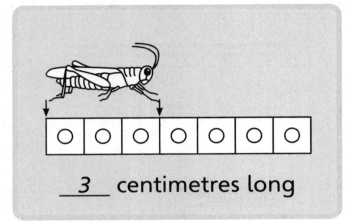 is I centimetre long.

☐ Write how many centimetres long.

___3___ centimetres long

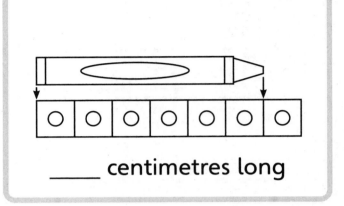

_____ centimetres long

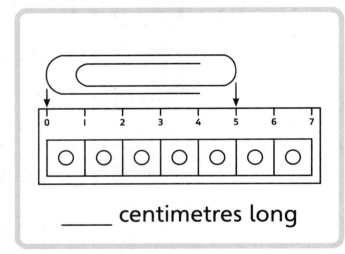

_____ centimetres long

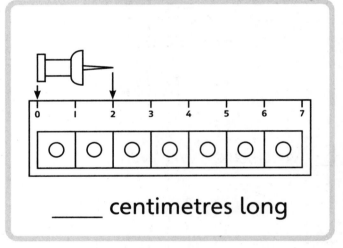

_____ centimetres long

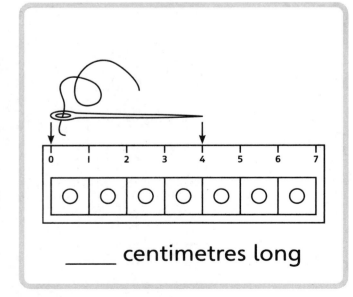

_____ centimetres long

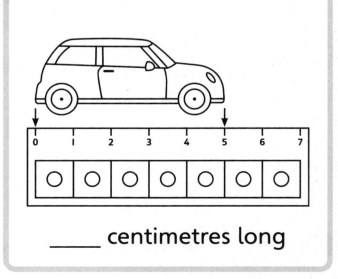

_____ centimetres long

We write **cm** for **c**enti**m**etre.

◯ Fill in the blank.

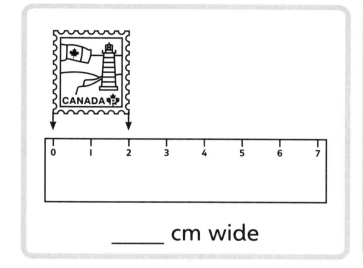

_____ cm wide

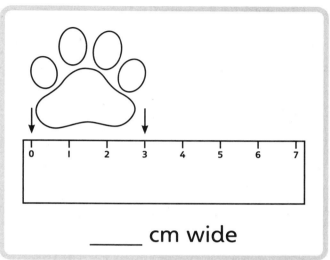

_____ cm wide

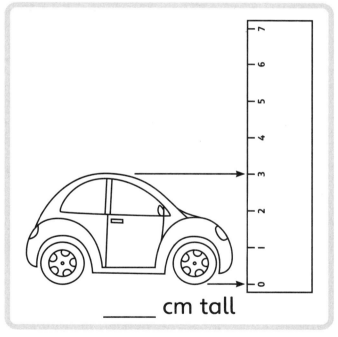

_____ cm tall

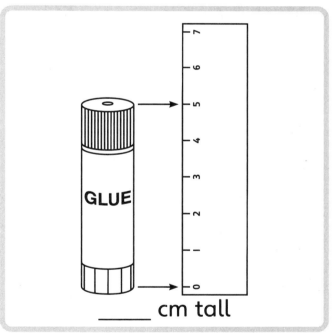

_____ cm tall

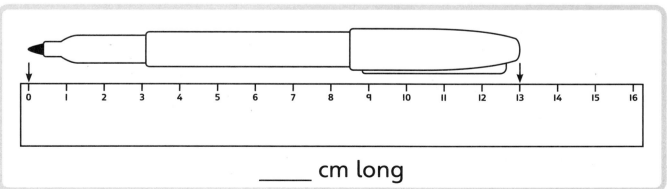

_____ cm long

☐ Measure the picture.

12 cm

0 1 2 3 4 5 6 7 8 9 10 11 12 13 14 15 16

Start at zero.

Start at zero.
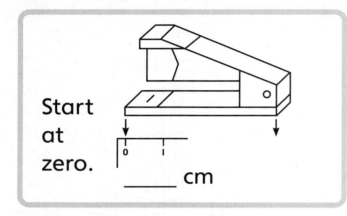
_____ cm

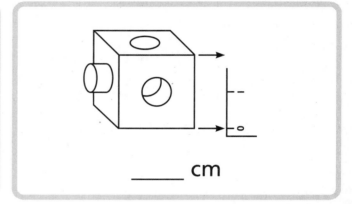
_____ cm

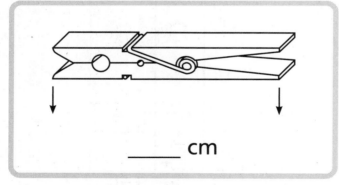
_____ cm

Start at both places.
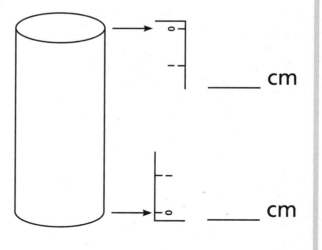
_____ cm

_____ cm

☐ Did you get the same answer? Explain why.

ERASER
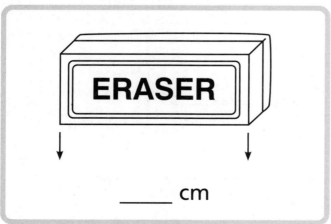
_____ cm

Measuring Using Centimetre Grids

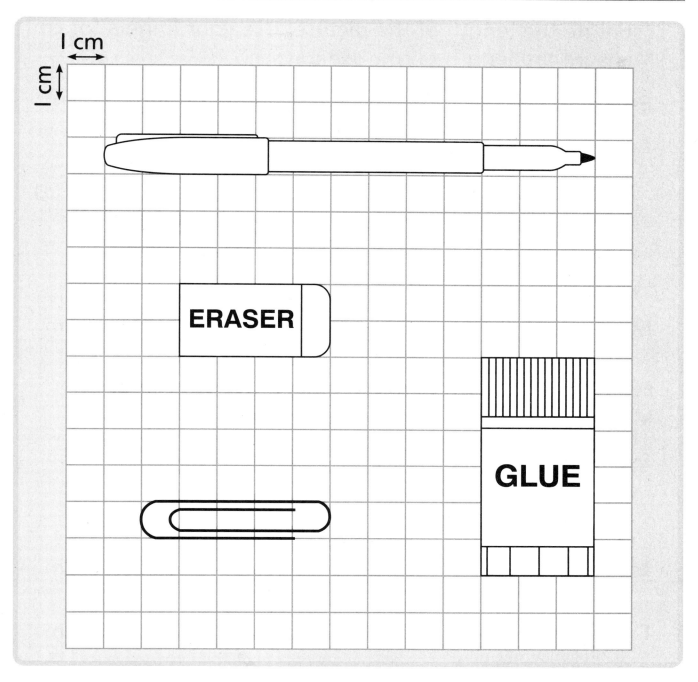

The ✏️ is ____ cm long and ____ cm wide.

The [ERASER] is ____ cm long and ____ cm wide.

The ⊃ is ____ cm long and ____ cm wide.

The [GLUE] is ____ cm tall and ____ cm wide.

Estimating Centimetres

☐ Estimate the length of the picture. Use your fingers for cm.
☐ Measure the length in cm. Use a ruler.

Estimate: about _____ cm

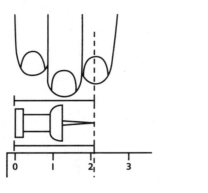

Measure: about _____ cm

Estimate: about _____ cm

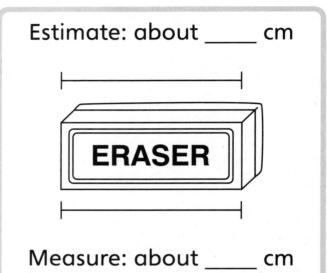

Measure: about _____ cm

☐ Estimate the length of a real object. Use your fingers.
☐ Measure the length in cm. Use a ruler.

Estimate: about _____ cm

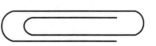

Measure: about _____ cm

Estimate: about _____ cm

Measure: about _____ cm

Estimate: about _____ cm

Measure: about _____ cm

Estimate: about _____ cm

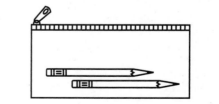

Measure: about _____ cm

▱ Are fingers a good referent for cm? How do you know?